MY DAILY RULES TO LIVE BY

Praise for

My Daily Rules to Live By

"I truly appreciate Dr. Weingarten taking the time to talk about his life's work. It is fascinating and I know it has helped many, many people. I wish him the very best as he continues his work. His passion to help others is truly remarkable!"

— *Mike Krzyzewski, Head Coach,*
Duke Men's Basketball

"Drawing on his rich life experiences, as well as distinguished learning, Sol Weingarten makes a compelling case for how his **Daily Rules to Live By** can change lives. This work lifts up a vision for renewed humanity that is accessible, practical, and life giving."

— *Rev. Peter Whitelock,*
Lafayette-Orinda Presbyterian Church,
Lafayette, California

"Dr. Weingarten's *My Daily Rules to Live By* helps people live better lives. As a social worker for over 25 years and after using My Daily Rules with many different clients, including prisoners, I have found it remarkably effective at stopping lower-level behaviors. Living at a 'Higher Level' is the ultimate goal of My Daily Rules, allowing us to have the kind of life we only dreamed of."

— *Paula Bosler, LCSW,*
California and Nevada

My Daily Rules to Live By

How to Become a Better Person

Second Edition

Sol Weingarten, M.D.

DUAL REALITY PRESS

Walnut Creek, California

Dual Reality Press
1966 Tice Valley Blvd. #175
Walnut Creek, CA, 94595
www.solweingarten.com

Two owls artwork by Andrew Denman
Original cover design by Mary Walker, graphic designer at Daily Digital Imaging; Updated cover for 2nd edition by Lorna Johnson
Interior Layout by Ruth Schwartz, aka The Wonderlady
Back cover photograph by Jeffrey Colhoun
Author photograph by Mike DiCarlo, courtesy of the
Rossmoor News
Book layout conceptualized by Allyson Edwards

About the cover: In the simplest terms, the two owls represent the two separate selves that all humans have.

Ordering Information:
Quantity sales. Special discounts are available on quantity purchases by corporations, associations, and others. For details, contact the "Special Sales Department" at the address above.

My Daily Rules to Live By/ Sol Weingarten, M.D. — Second ed.
ISBN 978-0-9974437-4-5 paperback
ISBN 978-0-9974437-5-2 eBooks
Library of Congress Control Number 2016937295

Dedication

To my beloved wife, Janet, whose work as an educator and a librarian supplied me with the research I needed and the encouragement to pursue this work, which she always supported up to her recent death. She made the creation of this book possible.

Acknowledgements

This book has been written during the past three years with the excellent help of several people. Allyson Edwards provided daily researching to ensure that everything in the book is as accurate as possible. James Alexander offered valuable insights into the qualities of human nature he experienced and witnessed as both an inmate and, most recently, as a talented psychologist. He has also written his own story in relation to the Daily Rules, which is featured at the end of this book. Robert Rosenbush helped me to get this project launched and maintained. Matthew Gilbert helped with his very fine editing. The residents of The Waterford in Rossmoor, California, where I live were enthusiastic participants over a series of meetings where I presented my work.

They showed that the benefits of the book's teachings are helpful to older people.

The book also benefitted from insights offered by many prison inmates who have described their transformative experiences in which they changed themselves from wrongdoers into productive, creative, and decent human beings. Several examples are included in the book.

People I've worked with from a variety of religious persuasions have shown me that all of them attempt to achieve similar improvements in the behaviors I have sought in my years of work. They have often been complementary, enhancing the benefits I have achieved with those I worked with.

My family members, including my father, mother, grandparents, sister, brother, and my deceased wives, all gave me the gift of caring, loving relationships. I have also been inspired by the success of nearly everyone I worked with in creating better lives for themselves and improved relationships with those around them.

The optimism I have for the potential of *My Daily Rules to Live By* to bring positive, transformative change to people has increased every year of my life and I acknowledge everyone who gives themselves this opportunity to become better people and to do good in their lives. At the same time, it's important to emphasize that The Rules will work differently for everyone, and are not intended to address serious psychological and emotional conditions. If you develop such conditions during your practice of The Rules, or continue to suffer from pre-existing conditions, contact a licensed mental health professional.

Table of Contents

Preface to the Second Edition

Welcome to this second edition of *My Daily Rules to Live By*. The response to the first edition has been gratifying, but I decided it was missing something important: a chapter on forgiveness. And so you will see in this new edition a new Chapter 6 entitled "On Forgiveness." While the suggestions in the first edition for improving oneself and becoming a better person prove to be very effective when practiced, the ability to forgive oneself and others for our damaging behaviors is another powerful tool for helping to create a better future.

The reality is that it's usually much too difficult for anyone to know exactly what is going on at any given moment during an encounter with another person. This prevents us from having enough information to make reasonable conclusions about what is happening and why, which makes mistakes and misunderstandings inevitable. As a result, we will often exaggerate trivial and even false impressions to rationalize what turns out to be our irrational behaviors and responses. If we want to maintain healthy relationships with both ourselves and others, even if we don't completely understand the nature of a particular disagreement or offense, being prepared to forgive becomes a necessary part of that process.

The benefits of forgiveness can be used by virtually everyone. The basic importance of being able to call upon ourselves to forgive when dealing with discord complements the rest of the suggestions in this book and may further contribute to your journey of becoming a better person.

Introduction

Everyone's life is filled with stories. We love good stories in books, movies, and even songs. They can help people relate to one another in ways they would never discover otherwise. Stories enable you to take a walk in someone else's shoes and get an image in your mind as to what the world is like for that particular storyteller.

In addition to other people's stories, we make up our own stories about the life we are living, as we live it. We play the role of hero and see ourselves with a sympathetic eye. For example, we might describe a co-worker in our story who makes a mistake on the job as lazy or stupid. However, when *we* make a mistake, our imagination produces a good (and often exaggerated) excuse, such as not getting enough sleep, missing the bus, or not yet having that first cup of coffee. In other words, it really wasn't our fault! These instinctively created rationalizations combine fiction and reality and are designed by "nature" to serve our prideful desires to make us appear good and completely right. Such stories show up in many of our interactions with others; they begin early in our lives and never stop.

This way of justifying our behavior would have benefitted our ancestors who were competitive predators — both eating and avoiding being eaten were necessary for survival. What they did *had* to be right. We have these same instincts, which unfortunately have often taken the forms of self-importance, conceit, and perceived self-competence, all of which are primarily prideful. They drive the belief — really the need — that we are 100 percent right and anyone who disagrees with us is 100 percent wrong. The stories we spontaneously make up, then, are meant to prove that "fact." They are distorted because they must show that we are completely right and the other person involved in the story or conflict is completely wrong.

In the civilized world of today, cooperation has become as important a human activity as competition. We co-exist with a wide variety of groups, both small and large, organized around different cultures, different religious beliefs, different sports teams, and so on. And while we are all "civilized" — wired in basically the same way — major conflicts continually arise. This has been true since the beginning of recorded history, including, more recently, two world wars and many regional conflicts that have led to more than one hundred million deaths in the past century alone. This unnecessary conflict and carnage occurs not just on global stages but between individual human beings. No matter how intelligent we are as individuals or in whatever groups we form, human conflict keeps occurring. In today's world, with the widespread accumulation of highly destructive weaponry, such conflict threatens the very future of the human race.

These dilemmas in human thoughts and beliefs brought *My Daily Rules to Live By* into being. Created over fifty years, while observing and working with thousands of individuals (with both good behavior and bad), the purpose of The Rules is to enable people to consciously stop themselves from behaving in destructive ways. It has been my experience that they provide a way for people to recognize their harmful impulses before they act on them. Those who've used The Rules have prevented bad behaviors and chosen instead to become more caring, creative, and decent people.

Such dramatic shifts don't necessarily happen overnight. They often occur gradually, evolving in the same way that The Rules themselves evolved. During my many years of practice, I paid close attention to which of my suggestions was most helpful to my clients (as they themselves would report) and I gradually compiled a list of the most effective, which ultimately evolved into **My Daily Rules to Live By**. They are literally "daily rules" and reflect the nature of personal change — an ongoing process of transformation rather than an immediate solution to all problems. Thus the importance of having realistic expectations; change will happen, but it will take time.

Nevertheless, virtually every human being who uses My Daily Rules acquires the tools to take charge of themselves — to consciously and voluntarily choose to control their behaviors. This is a huge step forward, for throughout human history people have been ruled by their powerful, instinctive selves rather than their own awakened consciousness. Imagine a world in which people related to others in such a way that those one hundred million deaths from violence never occurred, and where no one ever dropped a bomb that killed two hundred thousand people. Imagine a world in which the possibility of rising global temperatures was prevented by the joint actions of all nations and all peoples who brought conscious awareness to their actions. Practicing **My Daily Rules to Live By** will help make that potential a reality.

Chapter 1

How "The Rules" Came into Being

When I was twelve years old, my mother and father would often bring their near-violent disputes to me and ask for help. I recall their becoming calmer with each other when I was with them, relieved that they hadn't physically hurt one another. They would then get along reasonably well for a time until their next fight. And while of course I wanted them to get along and to have a good life together, I was aware that my mother would provoke his anger and I was afraid that my father was capable of hurting her.

When I helped them, I did so with love and without judging either them or the accusations of blame they heaped upon each other. I believe that I understood, even at age twelve, that while they were caring parents and responsible and decent citizens, their attacks and exaggerations were somehow automatic and reflexive rather than well thought out. I knew, even at that age (though I couldn't have known it consciously), that they were behaving as if each of them had two separate selves — one caring and loving and the other hateful and potentially violent. When I look back now, I see that the shift from being the best people they knew how to be to the worst form of expression they were capable of, seemed to happen in fractions of a second. How could that be?

As a retired psychiatrist who has worked with thousands of couples, I've concluded that none of them knew how to realistically be the loving partners or parents they wanted to be. What I encountered above all in my work is that when two people married, expecting to live "happily ever after," neither of them knew the difficulties they would encounter (whether or not they had children); nor did they have any idea that they would not be able to handle those difficulties in a kind and loving manner.

Fortunately, my parents were as lovingly support-ive as they could be to me and my two siblings as we were growing up. When we needed them for any health or school problem, they were always there for us. They provided for us and made plenty of sacrifices with their limited resources so we could all have college educations, which neither of them had gotten. And yet their own relationship was often stressful, which brought out qualities in me that I didn't know I had. It turned out these qualities formed a temperament that enabled me to care about and rarely get angry with the people I related to, no matter the circumstances. In my later years, when working with couples who had fierce disagreements such as those of my parents, this temperament helped me to see each "combatant" as having a caring, well-meaning self, no matter how willing they seemed to be to attack and destroy their partner.

When I was young, I had strong feelings of fear and insecurity, which prevented me from speaking until I was three years old. Fortunately, my mother realized that I understood whatever she said to me and patiently waited until I was comfortable expressing myself. This was a beautiful piece of parenting, intuiting that my delayed speech was a natural phenomenon and not the result of inadequate effort. She had very little schooling herself, having come to this country as a thirteen-year-old immigrant, the daughter of financially limited parents.

Thus, her good sense was independently available to her in the absence of traditional education.

My father, who also had very little formal schooling, suggested that I write a book explaining what I had learned about human nature. He did so when I had finished my training as a psychiatrist and was about to open my private practice. I told him that I did not yet have the experience that so many of my older colleagues had and thus would have nothing worthwhile to write about. He said, "Son, you have some understanding that they don't have, and it's worth writing about."

I appreciated his comment as being an expression of his love for me, and as I think back over my lifetime, I recall having always had this understanding spirit. Up until I was eighteen years old, I don't recall ever having had a fight with anyone. My attitude was one of respect for everyone who crossed my path. I believe I was born with a natural capacity to care for people and to help them deal more constructively with their anger. I found that being a psychiatrist gave me the opportunity to teach others to substantially overcome their tendencies toward damaging behaviors. I also recall having had a feeling of confidence that I would do well in whatever I undertook. The balanced self that seemed to bless me as a child enabled me to relate well to my parents and siblings, all of whom were different than I, and whose lifetimes were characterized by more conflict than mine.

People are able to see the temperaments of others even though they don't see their own. I know now, after working with so many people, that my own family must have noticed the way I carried myself, as it showed up in the tone of my voice and my emotions, actions and reactions, with them as well as with others. My attitude, above all, was to be respectful, and as a result I've had caring and conflict-free relationships with most of the people I've encountered. Realizing this gave me a set of standards and made me feel that I could help others achieve similarly respectful attitudes that would lead to similarly conflict-free living.

Also helpful has been my Judaic heritage, which goes back five thousand years and consists of ancient testaments that recorded the wisdom I was exposed to as a child. My grandfather was a Hassidic scholar who spent his life studying the scriptures. Hassidic scholars do not work for a living. They believe that their devotion to God will take care of them so they can disseminate wisdom to others. Studying their God to know him better directs such scholars to care about that God more than their own lives.

My father, who lived a practical, hardworking life as a tailor, was frustrated that his father didn't feel a need to work for a living, choosing instead to believe his religious beliefs alone would somehow take care of him. But this didn't necessarily apply to his children, which meant that my father had the burden of working from the age of twelve when he began studying to become a tailor. It was difficult and exacting work but enabled my father to support his three children, send them to college, and provide them with opportunities that he never had. For me it meant I had the good fortune to be supported for most of the twenty-three years of education it took to become a physician and then a psychiatrist.

Unfortunately, my grandfather and grandmother were killed during the Nazi Holocaust when I was a teenager. As a result, I never had the chance to meet and know my grandfather. The descriptions I had of him were of a decent, caring, and gentle person. When I asked my father to describe my grandfather and what he had learned as a religious scholar, he said that my grandfather believed that life was balanced and was meant to be understood. He would imitate the way my grandfather often replied to questions about his religious learning, holding one hand out as containing religious truths that could be achieved and the other hand as holding truths that still needed to be discovered. These gestures by my father helped me to feel that I knew my grandfather even though I'd never met him. I feel love for my father as well as my grandfather when I recall and re-experience how he shared with me the notion of balancing "on the one hand" with "on the other hand."

My War Experiences

When I was eighteen, I was drafted into the Army and became an infantryman in World War II. Because of my attitude of being respectful of others and expecting the same in return, I wondered what I would do when forced to become a warrior who might have to kill others or risk being killed by them. This was a very different self than I had been up to that time. I had three months of intense training at the army's "Infantry School" in Atlanta. I had no idea how that training would make me into a successful warrior, but I felt I would find a way, which somehow meant that I would survive. However, I was still fearful of what would happen in actual combat.

In thinking back to that time, I recall exactly what happened in my first battle experience. My regiment of a thousand men had waited an hour before the 5 a.m. signal to attack. During that hour, the enemy was being shelled by our artillery, stationed behind us and firing over our heads. I have never experienced such intense fear as I felt during that one-hour wait. While I was waiting, I suddenly heard a rifle shot a few yards away. I saw one of my buddies on the ground, writhing in pain, after having deliberately shot himself in the foot. I realized in that instant that he must have been as frightened as I was. When I saw what he'd done, I wondered if I should do the same — anything to overcome my overwhelming terror. I stopped myself. I figured he must have destroyed the bones of his foot and could end up crippled. I also felt a determination to fight as effectively as I could to help achieve victory against Hitler and his armies who threatened us with extinction. That thought, however, was extraordinarily faint in my mind. I realized afterward that my desperation to find a way out of fighting had taken over and made me forget, at least temporarily, what I was there for. Only by taking a moment of conscious awareness was I able to find the determination to go into battle and do the best I could. My buddy was hauled away and then we charged ahead.

I immediately experienced heavy artillery fire; when a shell landed near me, I could hear pieces of shrapnel whiz past me. When this happened at night, it was even more frightening — you could see the red-hot pieces of metal knifing through the air. During one such particular experience, when I was pinned down for three days with intermittent shelling that sometimes lasted for hours, I often felt like a cornered rat with no place to escape, reacting with the same life-threatened panic as everyone else who was fighting beside me.

However, the moment we started moving toward the enemy during that first combat experience, I was suddenly fearless. In fact, I felt an excited desire to fight. My complete being wanted nothing else than to engage the enemy. It was as though I was in a ball game, wanting to hit a home run. I felt a genuine desire to kill as many adversaries as I possibly could. Afterward, I realized I had no thought at all that my own life was in danger.

I remember watching a movie about warriors many years before my combat experience. I recall scene after scene of hand-to-hand combat using swords as weapons. The warriors in the movie all fought with enthusiasm and focused intent to kill their opponents. They also appeared to have no fear that they would be killed. I can say now that I was transformed in combat to be like those warriors, a person I never imagined I could be.

The point I want to make is that in asking people to stop their damaging behaviors, I am asking them to do what our ancestors fighting with swords would have been expected to do if given the order to stop. What I learned during my experience in the war was that, instinctively, I could kill others as purposefully as any other warrior at any time in human history. It's important to realize that in today's wars, soldiers are less numerous and the number of civilians engaging in battle has increased. We therefore make a mistake in thinking that only trained soldiers have a killing instinct — we all have that same instinct, capable of killing others and risking being killed. Living in to-day's world has changed our image of ourselves into thinking we've become civilized. We therefore live with an erroneous belief that we are solely conscious human beings who are naturally rational and peace-loving; we are instinctive warriors as well.

Back on the battlefield, I managed to hug the ground when shells landed or crawl to the bottom of a deep trench where I would have much less chance of being hit. One of my buddies in a nearby trench suddenly jumped out of it because he heard a friend call out that he'd been hit. He ran to help him, disregarding the danger he was in. I called out to him to hit the ground, but it was too late; the shrapnel of an exploding shell ripped him apart not thirty feet from where I crouched.

In thinking back to what happened, to what made a good soldier give up his life because he heard a friend call out for help, I realized that instinctive reactions such as the fear he experienced occur instantaneously, without any time taken to consider the consequences. In this case, it was the reality that running to help his friend during such a shelling was a suicidal mission. He would have had a much better chance if he'd crawled on the ground. We had been taught that if we were standing up when shells were landing close to us, the chance of being hit by shrapnel was 90 percent; crawling reduced that percentage to 20, while being in a trench made it 10. If we, as soldiers, had studied *My Daily Rules*, which did not exist at that time, more of us would have survived in the terribly dangerous situations we found ourselves in because we would have taken more time to think rationally about our options.

I never shared these stories after returning from the war because every time I recalled what happened, I felt overwhelmingly sad and helpless, as I did when I saw the horrible death of my friend. I have that same feeling now as I write these words; I not only see the face of my buddy but also his life situation. He was thirty years old, the oldest soldier in my company, and the only one I knew with children at home. He was a decent and warm-hearted person whose life was snuffed out in a second — which could just as easily have happened to me. Somehow my natural temperament gave me a better chance of surviving. Even when I was terrified, I remained disciplined and rational (at least as well as I could), which meant that I continued to be ruled by my sensible self no matter the situation, even when my survival was at stake. I believe it was a combination of temperament and luck that kept me from behaving in life-threatening ways.

About forty miles north of where we'd been fighting, another battle was taking place. It was called the Battle of the Bulge, because the Germans had succeeded in pushing the American troops back into a "bulge" of recovered lost ground. During that battle they took prisoners, and in a desperate attempt to frighten Allied soldiers, executed 183 of them.

I was in General Patton's army, and my division was used to draw the German attackers in while Patton's mechanized troops moved behind them so that eventually he could cut them off. His intelligence officers reported falsely to us that our battalion of one thousand men was to launch an attack against two hundred Germans who were holding a town called Orscholz and that we would have little trouble subduing them. Right before we set out to capture Orscholz — a week after the Battle of the Bulge began — my company engaged a German battalion in a nearby forest. We took forty-two German prisoners. After we captured Orscholz and felt we'd accomplished our objective, one of the lieutenants in my company ordered his men to execute those prisoners in retaliation for what the Germans had done to *our* prisoners. Fortunately for me I wasn't part of this retaliatory execution. The bodies were then left outside of town in a forest.

Three days later, we discovered that fifteen thousand Germans in a motorized division were just outside of town. (Patton was an effective and aggressive leader, and our division in his army became labeled as

"Patton's pawns.") They quickly overwhelmed us. A substantial number of men in my company were killed by artillery fire and most of the rest were taken prisoner. I managed to escape, fearful that I would be executed because I was Jewish, and eventually found myself in a group of five soldiers. We then encountered sixteen Germans. I was about to fire on them but one of the guys in our group suddenly stood up without his rifle, held up his arms, and called out that he was surrendering. I dropped my rifle and stood up to surrender as well. The Germans had discovered the weapon-less bodies of their comrades about two hundred yards from where we were captured. They could see that they'd been executed.

One of the Germans was pointing a machine gun at me, shaking with anger and yelling that I was an "American swine." At that instant I had an experience in which time slowed down so that every detail of what was occurring, every utterance by the German soldier, and every vibration of the machine gun he was pointing at me, were vividly ingrained into my consciousness. I then had the strangest experience of my life; I suddenly felt that I did not care if I lived or died. I knew there was at least a fifty/fifty chance that the German would shoot me, but I had no concern about that happening. I had no feeling at all about the continuation of my life. I experienced no fear. The thought of bullets tearing my body apart had no impact on me.

I realized afterward that this shift in my consciousness was automatic. It had nothing to do with any intentional action on my part to bring it about. My conscious mind no longer cared about the desirability of living that I'd assumed and projected before that gun was pointed at me. Later I thought of a story about the nineteenth century African explorers Stanley and Livingstone. Stanley was being mauled by a lion, but while his body was being tossed about as if it was a doll, he uttered no sound of panic or fear. He later said that he felt as though time had slowed down until finally someone shot the lion and saved his life. When that German soldier stopped pointing his machine gun at me and motioned me to the side of the road, I knew he wasn't going to kill me and the desire to live returned just as quickly as it had left me. I was now a prisoner of war.

By this time the war was nearing the end and prisoners weren't given enough food to survive for very long. There was little food for Germany as a whole and they weren't about to share much of it with us.

Instead they gave us rotten food and very little of it. We'd get sick, throw up, and have diarrhea. Many prisoners died of dehydration.

During this dreadful ordeal I saw something that really startled me. My fellow prisoners would steal from other prisoners who didn't have enough energy to eat. We were given one piece of bread every day, but many of us were too sick to eat it. Instead, we would place the bread under our heads as we lay on the ground to save it until we felt well enough to eat and to keep others from stealing it. However, some of the prisoners would find a way to steal that one piece of bread, which often led to others starving to death. This was a shocking experience for me. I could identify with the people who stole the bread because they were all starving, but I just couldn't do it myself. I was fortunate not to feel sufficiently desperate that I needed another's food to survive.

Still, survival instincts were driving us all at that point because we saw each other dying and knew that if we didn't get enough food, we would likely die as well. We shared the compound with Russian prisoners, many of whom died because the Russians hadn't signed the Geneva Convention at the end of the First World War that guaranteed prisoner's rights. The

Convention guaranteed that prisoners could not be made to work. The German forces went strictly by these rules, so while the Russians received the same food as we got, they had to work every day, and even the healthiest of them would die regularly. We were told afterward that a million Russian prisoners died in German prison camps.

What likely saved my life was the package of food that the Red Cross provided once a month for each prisoner. It was like a godsend. However, the Germans would sometimes give the packages to the prisoners to distribute, who would often steal some of them, leaving one package per month for four prisoners instead of one for each of us. Each package would have a pack of twenty cigarettes, and we'd end up selling five cigarettes to the German guards for a loaf of bread, which kept us going.

Gradually, a group of prisoners took charge of this terrible situation. Anyone caught stealing from another prisoner had his head shaved. This helped bring order and balance to the group because those who were responsible could now be recognized and controlled by the group. I asked some British prisoners who had been imprisoned for years how they had managed to survive. They told me that the same thing happened to them when they were taken prisoner. There was a period during the first few weeks when chaos reigned, and then a group took charge and restored some order. Recalling my religious training, I thought of Moses and how the Ten Commandments brought order to the chaos of the Israelites by providing rules for behaviors that were damaging to the group, such as *thou shalt not kill* or *thou shalt not steal.*

The capacity of people to change so much and so quickly the moment their situation changed — literally becoming two different people — baffled me. As soldiers we were buddies, cooperative and helpful, and this was especially true during the fighting. If I was running up a hill shooting at the enemy, someone could be counted on to cover me. But when I became a prisoner of war, some of my "buddies" were just as likely to steal the bread that kept me alive.

As the war neared an end in late May of 1945, the British army overran our prison camp and the guards fled. A reporter from *The Baltimore Times* came into the camp and began interviewing us, including me. He said if we wanted to have our names printed in our local newspaper at home to let people know we'd been released, he would forward our names to that paper. I described to him some of the situations we had suffered through and my name appeared in *The New York Times* along with the story. I hadn't realized that my family didn't know I was a prisoner. They did receive a telegram from the army saying I was missing in action but for several months they had no idea whether I was alive or dead. A cousin of mine noticed my name in *The Times* and phoned my parents. I was saddened to think about the ordeal they went through not knowing my fate.

A couple of days after being released, we were driven in army vehicles to an airport a few miles from the prison camp. We were then escorted onto transport planes that had no seats (which didn't matter to us!) and flown to Oxford in England where we were hospitalized and well fed for a few days. I had lost more than forty pounds but was in better shape than many of my comrades. From there we were sent to a U.S. base in Britain that housed landing ships for tanks, which had been used in the invasion of Normandy. The tanks were being sent back to Virginia and we joined them for a fifteen-day trip across the Atlantic. The food was good, the weather fine, and the voyage reasonably smooth. A bookcase on the ship was filled with paperbacks, which I read — one each day — finding relief and rest.

When we finally arrived in the U.S., we were given an eighty-day furlough to recoup from our ordeal in the camp, but the thought of returning as an infantryman again in a plan to invade Japan weighed heavily on us. Nevertheless, I prepared myself to go back in September when, in August, President Truman dropped two atomic bombs on Hiroshima and Nagasaki, killing almost two hundred thousand Japanese and bringing the war to an end. However awful the dropping of those bombs was, it saved the lives of thousands of American soldiers who would have invaded a country that believed surrender meant dishonor.

When I came home from the war, I found myself, like many of my comrades, unable to describe or discuss what I'd been through. I knew that I had fought well, helped my buddies, and done my best. But I also wondered if I could have done more, especially while a prisoner. When I brought this up with close friends who were prisoners with me, they pointed out that those who were the bravest were also the most likely to have died. They also suggested that those who had survived, including those who'd been prisoners, were both lucky and probably sensible in how they had handled the worst of the fighting. I was grateful to hear this, and to know that my fellow combatants had many of the same feelings I did. They, too, had no idea before actual combat how to deal with the fear of imminent death that was taking place all around them. It was impossible to know where and when the danger would come from. There was little we could control. It thus made little sense trying to replay or over-think the possibilities, probabilities, and uncertainties of how one might have fought in different situations. And yet that's what a lot of veterans do, which is part of the affliction called post-traumatic stress disorder (PTSD).

When in battle, one is focused entirely on both the dangers around them and opportunities to attack the enemy. Lose that focus for a moment and the likelihood of being killed goes way up. So we naturally become warriors if we wanted to survive. And nature assists us by making it much easier not to think or plan, which would slow down our process and make us more vulnerable. In battle, one must often rely on instinct to dictate the appropriate behaviors, and this happens automatically.

Once back home, however, in a civilized space where the use of guns is the exception, one becomes another person. So even though I enjoyed my expertise in weaponry, I decided to never possess a weapon again. When I think back to the war, I think about the German soldiers I fired at, seeing only the uniform and not the person in it. In a civilized environment, you see the person you're relating to and naturally recognize that person's humanity as the same as yours. One's experience in battle is thus very different than in normal society — you are literally not the same person.

I find that human beings are naturally kind and decent when their environment allows them to be that way. The fact that people can create civilized societies and live peacefully together helps prove to me that this is so. And so our dominant emotion is one of caring for others and wanting to help them. This is what soldiers with PTSD need to recall. In combat, they must *kill* the enemy, not care about them, and nature helps them do this. But when battle-worn soldiers return to civilized society, making the transition from warrior to peaceful citizen is challenging. Who they needed to be in combat is not who they naturally are and need to be in civilized society. I believe I survived the war because I had two extraordinarily important characteristics: I was able to be aggressive in battle when I needed to and to also care for others with compassion.

Still, returning home from the war at the age of twenty, I felt confused and disappointed that people could so easily have killed one another. I also came to realize that becoming courageous warriors with camaraderie of caring and a depth of feeling is a natural process when one is at war. I wanted to help humanity find a way to resolve this apparent paradox of behavior between natural aggression and natural caring. I decided to go to medical school to become a physician and a psychiatrist, which I thought would give me the training I needed. It started me on a long journey of working with many different sorts of people with all kinds of personal challenges, which ultimately led to developing **My Daily Rules to Live By**.

Becoming a Psychiatrist

When I finished school and became a psychiatrist, I thanked my father for generously supporting my studies. "Now," he said, "I want you to write a book about human nature."

His suggestion surprised me; I wondered how an "uneducated" man like him (except in tailoring) could judge my ability to have such knowledge. So I asked him, "How can I write a worthy description of human nature when there are many more people with so much more knowledge than I? I have limited experience and haven't even started practicing as a psychiatrist!" He replied, "I know that what you're saying is accurate, but regardless of how much training and experience people have, nobody has ever shown an adequate understanding of human nature.

"But I know *you*," he said, "and I know you can do it."

His confidence in me was a powerful inspiration as I set out on my quest. I have always believed that I'd be able to solve whatever problems came my way, and my father's attitude was even more helpful as I faced the uncertainties and challenges that all of us deal with in a lifetime of constant change.

During the first three years of my practice, I received further training as a psychoanalyst, was psychoanalyzed myself, and also worked with actual patients. Though my patients gained some understanding of their behavior, I was unhappy with the results. Our lengthy and laborious efforts did not bring about a significant enough change to warrant the time and effort that this analytic process required. I began to search for other approaches that promised to accomplish more in less time. I was fortunate to be practicing in the latter half of the twentieth century when new forms of psychotherapy were being discovered, and I explored them as they became available.

One of them was called "family therapy," developed by Don Jackson and Virginia Satir, who helped train me in the theory and technique. Their dramatic departure from traditional models consisted of open group expression rather than the private nature of psychoanalysis. The psychoanalytic process is devoted to helping the individual, while family therapy treats the whole family as a group. Along with other psychotherapists I would watch families undergo this approach through a two-way mirror. Tape machines in the room recorded everything that the therapist and the family expressed; these sessions would then be played back so that family members could hear their own spontaneous expressions. Watching these therapeutic sessions was a dramatic and effective form of psychotherapeutic training.

I recall one particular example in which a wife, hearing her recorded voice after a session, jumped up, pointed at the recorder, and blurted, "I did not say that!" In watching this take place, I realized that this woman must not have known what she was saying when she said it. All the other psychotherapists watching along with me laughed at this seemingly ridiculous reaction, but I remained silent. I later wondered what could have been happening in that otherwise intelligent woman's brain to make her react in such a self-contradictory way. She obviously heard her own voice played on the tape recorder. But when she realized that it didn't fit with how she felt at the time she heard it, she reacted as if it wasn't her — as if she was hearing a different person expressing beliefs that seemed foreign to her. She was automatically "saving face" without knowing it.

A similar process occurs when we look in the mirror; we generally feel as though the person we see is a stranger. This phenomenon of not relating to the image of our physical self or the words we hear ourselves speak indicates that our senses perceive ourselves as *two separate selves*.

Working with Couples

As I evolved as a therapist, I began to apply what I had learned about individuals and families to working with couples. After I'd seen about twenty couples who felt their only recourse was divorce, I realized that most of them began their session by expressing hatred for one another. This was very different from my experiences up to that point, in which I worked with only one person in separate sessions and sometimes with individual family members, including husbands and wives. With them I focused mostly on providing insight and suggestions for improving their ability to function in the world.

When a struggling couple came in, they were interested not so much in how I could help them to better communicate but on telling me what was wrong with the other person. Each one was determined to convince me that their spouse was a terrible person. They would try to make me into an expert witness who would agree that their partner was the most to blame for their problems. There was no way such hatred could be resolved at the level of these instinctive attacks. Further, while the couples were expressing their unrelenting hatred, they used mostly trivial issues to bolster their accusations, not realizing how superficial those issues were. I have found that this paradoxical misunderstanding is common in human behavior when two people are in conflict — especially for married couples who've been together many years. Their irritation with each other becomes more and more magnified to the point of convincing them that divorce is their only option.

As I sought to improve my therapeutic approach, I realized that I first had to wait until there was a break in a couple's cycle of mutual hatred. Then I would ask them a simple question: "How did each of you feel about your partner when you first met?" They each would take a moment or so and recall those early days. He might say, "I loved her smile" or "She was warm and friendly" or other feelings of caring and appreciation. She might say, "He was very open" or "He was so handsome and generous." They came up with many such recollections during the few minutes I had to encourage this looking back. And when this happened, the mood would change dramatically with a notable lessening of tension. At the end of the hour, I would generally arrange to see them again the following week. When they came back, they often showed a great deal more love toward each another. I realized that these changes in feelings represented changes in attitudes, which lasted for weeks and often led to the end of our sessions!

When I asked a couple to recall what took place when they first met, they had to take some time to remember. Taking that bit of time to consider their answer changed their conscious understanding of each other. They not only became a different person from the hateful self they were being but also realized that the person they were relating to was different than the one they hated when the session began.

In addition to discovering that couples *could* have such a sudden change in attitude, I had other experiences that added to my understanding of how such changes took place. Most importantly, it had a lot to do with how well they re-balanced their feelings of anger and caring, which is a more accurate picture of reality. In seeing one's partner as naturally imperfect, as having both good and bad traits, they got back in touch with both their caring selves that were present when they first met, as well as their hateful selves that would emerge whenever they were angered. They could see that those two separate sentiments were only partial truths as to who each of them really were. In seeing each other as they "really are," they would often fall back in love with each other. By simply allowing them to share their feelings of hatred with me — a neutral therapist — and then waiting for them to stop attacking one another, I was able to refocus them on a different, more positive, *and equally real* time in their lives.

This demonstrated to me that prejudicial feelings lead people to attack one another because they don't take the time to think about who they are attacking. Taking time is not what we ordinarily do when we are seized by strong emotions. I have found that being prejudiced by one's emotions rather than using one's reason and understanding is the most serious problem affecting all manner of human relationships, be they couples, families, between cultures, and even between nations.

Examples of Transformative Effects

One day my wife told me that she had read a short book called *Second Chance* by Syd Banks. I learned that Banks, born in Scotland, was not a therapist but a welder who had a natural interest in psychology and had a good friend who was a psychologist. One day while walking on the beach with this friend, he shared how insecure he'd been feeling because his relationship with his wife wasn't going well and his children had problems. His friend told him, "You're not insecure. You just *feel* insecure." As soon as he heard these words, he reported, he felt that he had suddenly been transformed. He found himself better able to deal with his difficulties by simply doing what he could about them but doing it more consciously. He felt he had a second chance in life to be a better person and decided to describe what happened to him so that others could also have another chance to become better people.

When I read this, I recalled that one of the things I taught my patients was the difference between feelings and reality. Feelings provide you with a sensation, which is a reaction to what you are experiencing. In this instance, Banks was responding with emotional instinctiveness to events that were taking place in his family. His friend told him that his insecurity did not reflect reality and that he needed to thoughtfully consider those feelings and the evidence for them. His subsequent transformation revealed something I didn't know about reality. As I look back now and having re-read his two books, I saw that his initial reactivity and the realization that followed reflected the reality of two completely separate selves. One of those selves judged his life and what was happening on the basis of how he instinctively felt about it, but the limited nature of that self doesn't describe reality. To be in reality, one must know that what is felt can be changed based on a different perception of an experience. When his friend juxtaposed his two separate selves, Banks suddenly understood that this was the nature of reality and it changed his life. His transformation occurred when he experienced the reality of two separate selves in one person.

It so happened that a group of psychotherapists had developed a therapeutic approach based upon Banks' discoveries and they were going to present it at a workshop close to where I lived and practiced. My wife and I attended to learn more about Banks' transformational process. During the break after the first morning session, I struck up a conversation with a social worker. After we talked a bit she said, "You know, I think you are the only psychiatrist here. Everyone else is either a social worker or therapist with far less training than you've had. Why would you come to a meeting like this?"

Without hesitation I instinctively blurted out, "I believe everything and I believe nothing." She looked visibly startled. I too was startled, until I realized that this was the driving force of my life up to this point. It just came out of me spontaneously in response to her question. I then began thinking about what the psychologist said to Banks that had brought about his transformation, and wondered if his assertion that there is a dramatic difference between *being* insecure and *feeling* insecure was made similarly off the top of his head. Was there a way to trigger such spontaneous utterances in my patients that would lead to a transformation in their self-understanding that would then carry over to the living of their lives?

Around the same time, I was seeing a patient who had lost her father when she was three years old. Now, at the age of forty-three with three teenage children and a successful life as a wife and a schoolteacher, she was in a persistent state of depression rooted in the loss her father. She had seen other therapists without success. At one point I reminded her that she was holding on to the *memory* of her father, who had been physically gone for forty years. She suddenly declared, "These are daily rules to live by!" When I asked her what she meant by that, she said, "I just need to keep reminding myself that he's gone." In the following weeks she did just that, and her depression improved. In checking with her several years later, she told me she was happier and more creative than she'd ever been.

This was the birth of *The* Daily Rules to Live By (which then changed to "My," as you will read in the next chapter). In my working with this woman, I simply acknowledged whatever she shared about her forty-year depression until she realized herself what she needed to do. I discovered that stopping someone's process of faulty reactivity long enough for them to see the larger reality of what is happening, results automatically in a transformation of perception that leads to a more evolved understanding. This showed that we all have a critically important instinct to get things right, which to me meant living in a reality where people care for each other as well as for themselves. This is exactly what occurs when people use My Daily Rules.

Breakthroughs with Prisoners

After using The Rules successfully with individuals and couples, I decided to see if they could improve the behaviors of hardcore inmates in California state prisons — a population that showed little success in efforts at rehabilitation. They generally spend years in prison without having changed themselves, and when they are discharged, 70 percent of them return to prison within a relatively short period of time.

When I worked at California's Solano State Prison, I introduced myself to groups of twenty-five prisoners as a psychiatrist who helps people change themselves — including prisoners. The tone and content of my introduction was an important part of the process. I let them know that my basic approach is one of acceptance and appreciation for having the opportunity to work with them. And by being a psychiatrist who also worked with people who hadn't been in prison, I was regarding them as being similar to those people. I wasn't judging them on the basis of their having done bad things; I was acknowledging them as being as capable as anyone of changing themselves for the better and doing good things. Most of the prisoners recognized this, and I found that the majority of them wanted to live a better life. They were often married and had children. Their successful use of The Rules would not only help them but would have an important impact on their families and their standing in their communities.

As you might imagine, working with prisoners is different than working with people from everyday society. And yet, the same capacity for transformation exists. The difference is not in the nature of their reactive instincts, such as fear, anger, and aggression — which we all share, but in the strength and power of them. In addition, those in prison are not just dangerous but are constantly living on an edge, wary of anyone who may belittle or attack or somehow take advantage of them. Walking into a prison to lead a session was always an intense experience for me. Prison can feel like a war zone; everyone there, inmates as well as guards, carries some level of tension. The atmosphere clearly isn't conducive to positive change.

Once that feeling of intensity wore off, though, I was usually able to feel comfortable, perhaps because I'd been in real war experiences, which were worse than anything imaginable in any prison. Also, my natural attitude was positive, an optimistic feeling that I was about to work with people who felt I could help. This attitude rubbed off on the people I worked with, which is the way of all attitudes (both good and bad) with all people. The prisoners were keenly perceptive and felt this, as they had plenty of practice assessing whoever came into the prison to help them. As a result, I actually had more dramatic results in my work in prisons than in any other setting.

Once a group of prisoners realized that my attitude of acceptance and caring was legitimate, they felt free to work with me. I would then begin the session with the following:

"I would like you all to answer a few questions, but don't answer immediately. Take some time to think about your answers before sharing them.

"First, in considering the rest of your life until you die, do you want to be a good person who treats others fairly and decently, a person who does good and is good? Do you want to have better relationships with your loved ones?"

Every group is quiet for about thirty seconds; you can literally hear a pin drop. Then about a third of the group begins nodding their heads, saying, "Yes." Another third haltingly says, "Yes." The rest of the group doesn't reply at all.

I would then ask those who hadn't replied whether not answering meant that they didn't want to be a good person who did good things. Many of them replied that they hadn't thought enough about the questions to have an answer. A few of them said that no one had ever asked them such a question. This would have conveyed to them that nobody expected them to ever be good.

I then asked the group, "With most of you wanting to be a good person, how is it that you did the bad behaviors that led to your being locked up in prison?"

The group answers *that* question without any hesitation: "I have a bad temper." "I'm a drug addict." "I didn't have enough money to get a good lawyer," among many other similar replies.

So I then asked, "Does that mean you are two separate selves? Could one of your selves be good and the other self one that does very bad things?"

I get several answers to this: "Maybe that's so." "I never thought about it." "That seems right to me." There is usually one person in the group who will suddenly exclaim, "I have been so evil!"

The first time this happened, I was surprised and asked, "Didn't you realize you were being evil?"

Many of those who responded in this way said that their actions "just happened" and that they had no idea how or why or even that they were hurting someone.

As I related earlier, when I was fighting in the war and intent on killing those who were trying to kill me, I felt as though I was firing at a uniform and not the person in that uniform. This apparently is natural human behavior, as I will explain later in the book when talking about the function and role of our amygdala, an important processing center in the brain. When we act instinctively, our behavior is automatic. We don't have time to know what we're doing when we do it. This is important to know because it means that the guilt we experience after having done something hurtful or destructive is, though understandable, misplaced. To improve those behaviors, they need to be dealt with realistically and from a larger perspective.

My Daily Rules to Live By

I would often think about what I'd learned from the prisoners I had worked with. I'd be walking across a prison yard and one of the inmates would invariably call out to me, "Hi, Doc!" Because I had worked with such large groups of prisoners over so many years, I generally wouldn't recognize the person who greeted me. "How are you doing?" I would reply. Virtually all of them had the same response: "I'm able to stop myself." They sounded proud of their newfound ability to stop committing bad behaviors. It seemed they were also saying that they felt good about themselves and were proud to be a good person. When I asked them to tell me more, they let me know of positive attitudes and decent things they had done. These were not experiences they would have had while growing up; The Rules changed their lives and behavior for the better.

One example of a positive behavioral change was in how they corresponded with their families. Usually their letters were filled with complaints that their families weren't sending them enough money, which they used to purchase small comforts that helped make their lives in prison more bearable. They would also demand more visits even though their families didn't have enough money for travel. After practicing The

Rules, the criticism and complaints began to subside. They expressed more appreciation for the sacrifices their families had to make because of their incarceration and inability to provide for them. There was also more appreciation for their family's caring despite all the misery they were experiencing. In short, they appreciated *living in reality* and were happier as a result.

One of the prisoners I worked with who was serving a life sentence without parole for murder, lost any desire to commit violent behavior. Instead, for the first time in his life, he discovered an interest in learning and attended school classes in the prison. After three years he became an assistant to the electronics class teacher. When I asked how he felt about the rest of his life knowing he would spend it in prison, he replied, "I've never been happier." His transformation appeared complete and permanent.

A number of other prisoners I worked with became interested in learning. They took advantage of what the prison could offer (some actually have small schools) and also took correspondence courses — which they had to pay for — that would help prepare them for employment once they got out. Those with life sentences and no possibility of parole, such as the inmate I mentioned above, also changed for the better as they sought out opportunities for learning and self-improvement. They were able to experience their better selves and function as more decent human beings.

It seems magical that people can completely transform who and how they are for the rest of their lives no matter their circumstances or history. They are capable of naturally and automatically choosing to be better people without having to do anything but perceive the bigger reality that The Rules reveals to them. These remarkable changes have made me realize that potentially every person on the planet can benefit from The Rules in bringing about deep and lasting change.

Chapter 2

Introducing "My Daily Rules"

I have a natural desire to help people and am open to exploring whatever they bring to me, both good behaviors and bad. I have found that everyone I've worked with has a natural wisdom within their minds, and I have learned from that wisdom during my sixty years of therapeutic practice. It has enabled me to develop **My Daily Rules to Live By**, which have helped nearly everyone I've worked with to improve their behavior and live fuller lives. I have always asked the people I worked with to share their experience of The Rules with me, and in so doing I continued to fine-tune them so that they better described the reality that people live with.

A dramatic example of how such feedback shaped The Rules happened while I was working with seven prisoners being held in solitary confinement. Each one had a separate, cage-like structure with a tiny seat on which they could sit for the hour-long session. This prevented them from hurting one another or anyone who worked with them, including me. I would stand in front of the cages and speak directly to them.

During one of our group meetings, a prisoner suggested that rather than "*The* Daily Rules," it would be better to call them "*My* Daily Rules."

"How come?" I asked him.

He replied, "Nobody else could be as stupid as I was to kill somebody because they looked like they didn't respect me!"

When he said this, I immediately realized that he was right. Everyone needed The Rules, but they needed them to be *their* Rules. They needed to realize that The Rules applied to their own patterns of hurting others. Everyone I've worked with is naturally prideful, and we all react strongly, for example, to not being respected. We can overreact to even the slightest trace of disrespect. This emotional reaction happens automatically and instantly. In addressing such behaviors if they become habitual, My Daily Rules become a personal reality for anyone who uses them. They pertain specifically to the user of The Rules and what will work for that person.

I replied to the prisoner who made the suggestion that each of the other six prisoners must feel the same way. I said to the group, "If you use The Daily Rules to help yourself become a better person, you must learn that you have your own way of hurting someone for a stupid reason. They really are 'My Daily Rules,' and you will need to use them every day of your life to stop repeating behaviors that haven't worked for you in the past."

It's important to reiterate that we all share the same emotions and a capacity for similar misbehaviors, but we are completely different in the frequency and intensity of how we carry them out.

I realized during that session that these seven prisoners had misbehaved in prison in a way that justified solitary confinement, and that those behaviors were likely similar to the ones that got them arrested and sent to prison in the first place. I also saw that merely explaining The Rules gave rise to the suggestion that they should be personalized. These prisoners were changing simply by learning that these Rules existed, and as they heard them being described, they immediately began to relate to them. As further evidence that The Rules were having a positive effect, two veteran officers grudgingly admitted that the seven prisoners seemed to be changing their behaviors as a result of my sessions. Such officers usually have years of experience during which they never see prisoners "change their stripes," and so their acknowledgement of a change was strong evidence that even hard-core prisoners were capable of transformation.

This is how "My" Daily Rules came into existence as an outgrowth of "The" Daily Rules, thanks to the important contribution of an inmate. They are an evolving set of guidelines for preventing destructive behavior patterns. They begin by instructing the person using them to thoughtfully create a list of behaviors that have been damaging to themselves or others in the past, such as irrational expressions of anger, exaggerated fear, persistent worry, vengeful acts, substance addiction, or other self-damaging tendencies. These I have associated with our "Lower-level" self. As a result of practicing The Rules, you will discover and reconnect with your "Higher-level" self.

My Daily Rules to Live By
by Sol Weingarten, M.D.

These rules are tools that enable me to control my harmful impulses in order to be the person doing good that I want to become.

1. In order to know which impulses to control, I am listing below my **Lower-level** thinking and behaviors that have done damage to me and others:

_____

_____

2. I will also record situations that trigger my damaging Lower-level behaviors:

_____

_____

3. When I experience these Lower-level impulses or feelings, I will say to myself:

   - ***STOP!***

   - I am at a lower level

   - I must not act upon these impulses

4. Stopping my damaging Lower-level behaviors **automatically** frees me to become my **Higher-level** self.

5. Everyone's observing self, as well as my own, is always experiencing concern about being criticized, not respected, or being treated unfairly. Therefore, my Higher-level self must **always** be ready to recall that:

   - My Lower-level self must let go of my prideful reactions of anger, fear, or jealousy.

   - I also must let go of hurt feelings before they do harm to myself or to others.

- My Higher-level self will respect everyone no matter how badly I am being treated.

- I also will respect them because I know with certainty that every one of us can behave badly, but that we all want to be good and do well in life.

- I will practice being aware of what I say or do, **as it is happening**, rather than after.

Reviewing these rules every day will cause them to become automatic behaviors and second nature to me.

Higher-Level State of Being

In this state of mind, my purpose becomes to do good and be good, no matter the circumstances in which I find myself. My Higher-level self gives me the ability to **choose** my improved behaviors.

At a higher level, my attitude becomes:

1. *Knowing* the consequences before acting

2. Patient by taking time

3. Thankful and generous

4. Steady and balanced

5. Responsible and self-controlled

6. Courageous and tough-minded

7. Curious to learn

8. Positive and considerate

9. Sympathetic and forgiving

10. Fair-minded by being *compassionate*

11. Respectful of *everyone*

Higher-level awareness enables me to:

1. Stop myself from harmful behaviors

2. Become smarter and more creative

3. Discover my common sense and seek honest advice

4. Be politely firm but always respectful

6. Allow my higher-level to preside over my lower-level

5. Find joy and contentment no matter what setbacks life brings

6. Find a strong sense of peace of mind

7. Choose what is *right* for me and others

© 2016-2017 Sol Weingarten, M.D.

My Daily Rules to Live By

Following the instructions of Rules No. 1 and No. 2 reveals which behaviors need to be stopped. We are all prone to react instantaneously and emotionally whenever we have a disagreement or feel provoked. Emotions such as anger, fear, and worry affect our mood and our attitudes and trigger our instinctive behaviors, which can do damage to ourselves as well as others. These instincts are designed by nature to react instantaneously without us having to think about them. Rule No. 3 stops these emotions before they cause harm, helping one to become more thoughtful and civilized, and able to stop their "warrior self," for example, when fighting others isn't necessary. When "The Rules" became "My Rules," they became more applicable to each individual's unique situation.

Some of the most frequent examples of emotions and behaviors that, in my experience, people have identified as needing to be stopped are the following:

1. **Anger** — "Stop!" at the first sign of feeling *irritated* or *bothered*. An example is a parent in a bad mood who punishes a child for making a trivial mistake.

2. **Fear** — "Stop!" fears such as anticipation of having to speak in public, which is an overreaction to

the trivial danger of being criticized. Speaking in public generally won't cause harm even if one makes a mistake. *Shyness* is another manifestation of fear experienced by virtually everyone. Practice speaking up in groups, for example, by asking questions. This enables one to get more comfortable in freely expressing feelings and ideas without fear of criticism.

3. **Pride** — "Stop!" reactions such as unnecessary competitiveness in cooperative tasks with family members and classmates. Also, when a child's school performance needs help, explore together how to improve it rather than express disapproval. And if one sibling is better at a sport than another, stop any teasing or comparisons. A lot more will be said about pride in Chapter 5.

4. **Worry** — "Stop!" unnecessary concerns about future outcomes that lead to preoccupation with excessive worrying. Spending time imagining potential disasters or loss is more often hindering than helpful. The future is always at least partially unpredictable and most people tend to have exaggerated worries, which don't tend to help generate useful conclusions. It's better to simply consider if

there is anything that can or needs to be done, and then doing it.

The key to living in a civilized society is knowing that we are two separate selves: an instantaneous self and a self that takes time before acting. Nature has designed them both to give us two sets of unique and valuable strengths. It seems strange, though, that we don't naturally recognize that these two separate selves exist. This ignorance is part of the reason our instincts have had such influence. It's time for that influence to be reversed so that our thoughtful self is more in charge. Each individual change then helps to improve the entire human race.

Because the two selves are experienced as one, we switch in an instant from one to the other without knowing this is happening. We can go from being calm and caring to angry and even murderous. This served our human ancestors well in their daily struggle for physical survival, but those conditions have obviously changed and The Rules help us to separate those two selves when we consciously use our own minds.

In today's civilized society, we no longer have to kill other humans to survive or to keep from being killed (except, of course, when our survival really is at stake) because for the most part we've learned to stop ourselves. In so doing, we in fact become a different human being, a more conscious self that automatically takes time to take charge of our behaviors. I call this more conscious self our "Higher-level self," which has been purposely designed by nature to enable us to live with kindness and consideration. With practice we find that we automatically choose these better behaviors without us having to think about them.

When prisoners first become aware of My Daily Rules, most of them realized right away that they apply to them and also how they apply. Their previous behaviors were triggered in similar ways to what happened to me during the war and to our ancient ancestors when protecting their families from predators. Each situation was life or death, kill or be killed. Of course, in the case of these prisoners, the threats triggering their sometimes murderous response usually weren't life threatening, but they instinctively thought they were.

And so if we are to control the behaviors that do damage to ourselves, to others, and to society — which I call the actions of our Lower-level selves — what rules would we need? What could people apply on a daily basis to successfully manage their destructive impulses? My answers, developed over many years of practice and experience, are **My Daily Rules to Live By**.

Over the years that I was developing My Daily Rules (thanks again to the help of prisoners and other patients who realized they needed to change themselves), I saw the similarities of today's world to the world of the Ten Commandments. They came into being thirty-five hundred years ago to control the chaos that beset the Israelites during the time of Moses. The world has changed dramatically in those thirty-five hundred years but people still need instruction on how to manage their behaviors. I see My Daily Rules as a kind of modern update to the more restrictive rules that were needed at the time of those commandments.

We know that "commandments," standards, and rules of behavior have changed over the thousands of years of recorded human history, and I expect there will be more revisions to come. *The Ten Commandments*, for example, were appropriate to the people living at that time, and yet our basic emotional makeup has changed very little. We know, for instance, according to National Geographic's Genographic Project, that today's human DNA includes one to four percent of the same DNA found in our Neanderthal ancestors forty-to-fifty thousand years ago. And so one of my main purposes in developing **My Daily Rules to Live By** was to make them relevant, both today, and for as long as the human race exists, because we still have a lot of work to do to avoid the pitfalls of other species that came to the end of their evolutionary journey.

The test for any revisions that take place in the future is that they must be "realistic," meaning they must reflect and be adaptable to the changing world that human creativity keeps bringing into being, even though the human race itself has not evolved as rapidly as its technological accomplishments. Realistic means that if the human race has weaponry that can destroy the world in a matter of hours, it must also have the rules and realistic ability to keep that from happening. So far we seem to be achieving that goal; immense destructive power has been available for seventy years — fifteen thousand atomic bombs possessed by nine different nations. Will those nations continue to be led by people who understand the danger and the issues at stake? Can The Rules influence the ideologies of those countries so that despite their differences, which are a constant source of conflict, situations don't escalate to a globally destructive end game?

Seventy years is not long enough to assure that subsequent generations will be free of the threat that these ideological differences will continue to pose. However, The Rules can rapidly bring about the kind of individual change in attitudes that can overcome these differences and help preserve the future of the human race. People want to be good and to be good to others — that is their natural state of being. Humanity's evolutionary progress shows its enormous creativity and potential. Combined with the thoughtfulness and the reality that My Daily Rules provide, we have the power to overcome these conflicting ideologies, allowing us to relate to and accept one another with the essential goodness we all share.

Chapter 3

"Stop!"

What I have found in working with large numbers of people is that My Daily Rules help them see that they are able to become very sensible. They realize that by stopping themselves from repeating previously damaging behaviors, they will have much better outcomes in the future. The challenge is that each new situation triggering strong emotions feels just like that — new and different, as if we have never had that particular emotion or situation before.

We've all had fears, angers and worries in the past, and we can recall behaviors in various situations that didn't turn out well because of them. A *new* situation that is similarly challenging may present us with different problems, but we'll likely respond with the same intense focus and instinctive reaction that produced bad behaviors in the past, because in the heat of the moment we don't remember those previous experiences. That's the way instinctive behaviors work.

Our natural self is not designed to do any thinking before reacting to a disturbing situation. The focus is placed entirely on what is bothering us — the "enemy" that we're encountering. Whatever strong emotion we feel captures all of our attention and automatically takes charge of what happens in our mind. Because instinctive behaviors are so fast, we don't realistically consider what's really going on and we make mistakes, many of which are very stupid, and some of which send people to jail. And because we always want to be right in whatever we do, our mind produces a "corrected" version, a "story," of what occurred. These stories are automatically exaggerated because no matter the circumstance, we have trouble accepting that we made a mistake, especially when important issues are at stake. We imagine the worst possible punishment and we panic, doing anything to avoid it. And so our instinctive reactions are automatically driven both by thought and feeling, which become completely focused on any potential threat that is worrying us, angering us, or causing us fear.

Take the example of road rage. When someone cuts in front of us, we are automatically angry at whoever is driving that car. This occurs even when we can't see the driver. It happens so quickly that even if a car were self-driven, the same rage would be experienced. The source of this instantaneous anger is the amygdala, which is located in the temporal lobe deep inside the brain. The road rage one feels is instinctive and happens in less than a tenth of a second. It makes us into a separate self with the sole desire to express our rage verbally and physically. The same thing happens with fear, such as when a caveman facing a tiger runs first and thinks later.

Recent studies have found that humans have the capacity for subliminal recognition: when the mind "measures" what it sees even if we aren't consciously aware of seeing it. Instinctive behaviors are thus subliminally informed and automatic in nature; they don't need to cognify what and who they are reacting to, such as what happens in road rage. In the animal kingdom, an example of what I'm describing is the behavior of cheetahs, whose instinctive minds judge their environments and behave in ways that enable their survival. As described in a 1986 *Scientific American* article, "The Cheetah in Genetic Peril," cheetahs make realistic judgments of their success in catching a potential prey using complex mathematical measurements to calculate the distance, angle, and speed of motion of their target. They instinctively know they can run seventy miles per hour for a short period of time, for example, and that antelope can run only sixty miles an hour but for a longer stretch, so they instinctively consider all factors. This ability to *measure* increases the frequency of a successful hunt.

The same mathematical measurement occurs in the human mind as well. The great discoveries of Newton and Einstein began with an instinctive appraisal of the mathematics involved in gravitational effects and relativity. It was only *after* they made their intuitive observations that they used formal statistical means, such as calculus and the mathematics of curvature, to confirm the reality their minds had measured.

We are similar to other species in responding to things we recognize while observing our environment — a reaction that occurs in less than a tenth of a second — but unlike other species, those observations can trigger spontaneously strong, negative, and often prideful emotions. When that happens, we automatically and unconsciously make up exaggerated stories that justify our behaviors about those feelings using information that is stored in our memory, providing meaning without the need for conscious consideration. This is the non-conscious state of mind we live in most of the time. It enables us to react instinctively without having to think about what is happening. In situations of perceived threat *or* opportunity, it protects us without our having to take precious time to figure out what we're protecting ourselves from or what kind of story is behind the opportunity. In the example of a spider waiting for its prey, it acts automatically and without hesitation as soon as it recognizes that prey is caught in its web. While the spider is waiting for its opportunity, it must also be on the lookout for predators, including humans with a flyswatter.

All the information that the spider draws from in that process of recognition and response is similar to the information that our own minds have when we react with strong emotion to certain situations. This mode of reactive consciousness reveals a separate and different person than the conscious self that would take the time to think about what it's perceiving. The "primitive perception" that our instinctive mind makes — and acts on — feels complete, as though we know what we're doing when we do it. We need no other information to direct our actions and behaviors. Our brain automatically makes up a story for us. In effect, the story writes itself. We are not conscious participants in the process.

These instincts are rooted in our genetic prehistoric nature, which our brain has access to. Going back to my therapeutic work with couples, in a typical example they would generally begin our session by being hateful toward one another. When I asked them to describe what was behind these emotions, each would blurt out exaggerated examples of their partner's terrible behavior. I came to realize that these intense emotions were being instantly expressed without their taking time to consciously consider what they were hateful about. They were responding from within that one hundred-millisecond time frame, preventing them from thinking more consciously about the person being criticized — or their own emotions. All they felt was how despicable that person was. It was as if they were battling a deadly adversary they had to defeat.

It was difficult to interrupt them with constructive observations or suggestions. I would have to wait until the battle came to a temporary halt and then ask them to answer a question. As I wrote earlier in the book, it was to stop for a moment and recall what they felt about one another when they first met, during that exciting time when two people are getting to know each other and experiencing that initial attraction. Considering this question changed their attitude. Instead of looking strained and intensely preoccupied, they visibly relaxed. Such relaxation needs a bit of time and conscious awareness to occur, but once it happens, their change in stance and in attitude automatically and spontaneously shifts. The hateful people they were suddenly cease to be. Instead, they become the people they were when they first met, alive with the positive feelings and emotions they had years ago. They see each other once again as caring, friendly, and attractive. The following week they would return as a very different couple, in love as never before. I wondered how such a dramatic transformation could occur merely by taking an additional half-second to consider a larger story.

As I considered this fight-to-the-death phenomenon, I began to realize that when two people share the same angry and hateful state of mind, they see each other as enemies and automatically do whatever it takes to attack them and win the battle. They have no memory that the person they are fighting was ever a worthy friend. Their minds worked the same way mine did as an infantryman fighting in a war, primed to kill the enemy without hesitation. I felt no need to consider anything about the enemy that would have made them seem worthy or decent. I had absolutely no caring for that person; they were trying to kill me so I would kill them first. This is the warrior state of mind and everyone on those battlefields had it. Looking back, it made me realize that we all have within us that warrior self as well as a conscious and caring self. These two separate states of mind, when juxtaposed, are able to work as if they are one within our single mind-body self. This takes place without our conscious awareness. Our consciousness is unable to differentiate the tiny amount of time between the instantaneous reaction of our primitive selves and the extra half-second it takes to connect with our more caring and conscious self. And so in our experience, the two selves feel like one, though the reality is that there are two separate minds at work.

This is the work of nature, enabling us to be both purposefully caring and a purposeful warrior, who can kill if necessary. Each separate self is capable of being completely engrossed in one or the other state of mind. The couples I worked with were only able to know themselves and their mates from a bigger perspective when they took the time to think about those past selves and compare them to the hateful ones they were expressing.

Taking Time to "Stop!"

The reactions we have within that first tenth of a second reveal a non-conscious self, which can look and act very different than the self that emerges a half-second later. And yet, most of us don't realize that we become that non-conscious self the instant we have a strong feeling — and that we can get stuck in that self. This lack of insight fools us into believing that we know what we're doing, and that our emotional actions don't need to be questioned. Thus when two people argue, they keep cycling through a process of instant, righteous, back-and-forth attacks. The anger they're expressing *feels* entirely justified because the self they've become knows nothing but the anger being expressed. The reality is that we have no conscious knowledge of what is taking place when emotions like that our triggered. We are reacting naturally and automatically without feeling a need to think about it. Our considerate, caring self becomes a bystander to the power of our instinctive self. Instinctive behaviors do not rely upon intelligent thought; they respond instead to our genetic instruction.

Whenever people — including our leaders — operate from a place of anger or fear, their decisions will not be made with conscious consideration; they will instead be ruled by the instinctual urgency behind that emotion. This was generally true for the prisoners I worked with. When I described the amygdala's function and the time difference between an instinctual and a thoughtful perception, they would often realize how "stupid" they had been to have become enraged enough to kill someone *before* they had time to know what they were doing. They discovered for the first time that their angry reactions and the results that followed were initiated without prior thought or consideration, and that the situation could have turned out differently.

We all assume that we're at our best whenever we have a strong feeling about what we want to do. That's true when we passionately devote ourselves to something useful, such as getting a college degree or starting a new business, but those same strong feelings can lead to terribly damaging behaviors. When this happens, we don't realize we've been reduced to a primitive state of mind with primitive judgments.

Those powerful primitive emotions aren't all bad, of course. Joy and love, for example, are highly positive. Even fear and anger can provide useful signals for how to respond in a given situation. The "primitive state of mind" simply generates strong feelings that can end up being good or bad depending on what we do with them. And that's the critical point: My Daily Rules harnesses our free will, which stands apart from most other species, to stop behaviors that do damage to ourselves or others. The Rules have been constructed so that, in Rules No. 1 and No. 2, you list patterns of damaging behaviors you've done in the past. It takes just a bit of conscious time to recall such behaviors. Rule No. 3 instructs you to simply "Stop!" whenever you experience an emotion that is about to repeat a damaging behavior. All that's needed is to pause for half a second and consciously choose to take charge of your behavior. The decision to stop yourself gives you immediate access to your conscious mind, your Higher-level self, which will act on the order and stop all the energy that would otherwise fuel the damaging behavior. When this happens, a transformation in behavior automatically takes place as you are now operating from your more evolved self.

Our mind's ability to stop instinctive behaviors is rooted in information provided by DNA molecules in the brain. Recent discoveries in epigenetics have shown that genetically determined behaviors can be stopped by turning off certain gene switches that are associated with those behaviors. There are twenty thousand genes in these DNA chemical molecules, which instruct and shape our behaviors *and* enable us to be aware of them as they are taking place. Nerve cells make up the brain, while the cells in the rest of our bodies transmit information about what's happening in the areas *they* occupy. However, what's different about brain cells is that they also control the behaviors of our organs and physical structure. These behaviors occur automatically, initiated by our non-conscious minds, which instinctively allows them to function and react without any need to think about which ones we want to express. Only when the mind *chooses* a behavior is it operating consciously.

This "DNA self" is chemical and robotic in nature. It doesn't experience itself as a conscious living person, nor does it relate to others as if they have legitimate, conscious feelings. One can say that it's unconscious or non-conscious, but literally it has no conscious mind to thoughtfully consider the true nature of a situation.

The behaviors that emanate from this chemical self occur instinctively and have a chemical, molecular feeling that is *experienced* as ongoing. This means it has no concern when death seems imminent — unlike our conscious self that is very aware when its life is at stake. Thus, in battle, warrior selves are able to fight and kill other humans as if both are chemically inanimate creatures. Even citizens who support a war can become this inanimate chemical self with only passing concern for the fate of the combatants while they deal with their own life dramas. Our instinctive actions, therefore, take place with the same lack of consciousness that characterize the instinctive behaviors of other creatures. They are, literally, robot-like and unconscious. This helps explain the strange phenomenon of attitudes that are both conscious and non-conscious, reflecting two completely separate selves that live in every single one of us — two sets of attitudes that are separated from each other by the time it takes for the amygdala to process information.

When I first started introducing My Daily Rules to groups of prisoners, I was surprised to discover that some would blurt out that they had been "evil." This would happen after they'd taken the time to consider whether they wanted to be good people doing good things and deciding that they did want to be those people. Previously to learning about The Rules, they felt that other people were evil but not them. Discovering The Rules and facing the hard reality of their past actions, they realized they must be built in such a way that they instinctively acted in an evil manner. This insight gave them new a perspective; they were seeing themselves and their actions for the first time within a larger reality. They realized that they must be two separate selves, each with different ways of behaving: one self could be terribly damaging, while the other self wanted to be kind and decent. And these two selves seemed to be strangers to one another. They were surprised and even shocked at learning this, and yet the realization of it appeared to shift their attitudes. This was a critical turning point, because it gave them insight into how things went wrong and also a powerful tool to prevent them from happening again. And for many of these prisoners their lives did change for the better.

This is the great transformation that takes place when one simply says "Stop!" to the behaviors of one's Lower-level self. And it takes very little energy to do this. Molecules of DNA are very small and use only the tiniest of energies to fuel our conscious thinking activities. The power of the human mind therefore requires very little effort to initiate major activities. The idea that the molecules of the human brain are so remarkably efficient is relevant to understanding the miraculous nature of the mind. The half-second it takes to pause and consciously choose to stop a damaging behavior not only uses the least possible energy but enables us to access and consider most of the information stored in our memory: useful information, effective information, realistic information. Information not about the way we feel but about what we know. The human mind innately knows what is right and what is good. It wants to behave well. All it needs is the awareness to make good choices about which destructive behaviors need to be stopped; nature will then replace what is stopped with better options.

Pearls of Wisdom

Bob, retired architect

By way of introduction, my name is Bob. I'm an architect and have had a very difficult life because of bad feelings about myself. I'm now eighty-two, and had an unexpected moment of clarity when first hearing **My Daily Rules to Live By** described at a meeting I attended in early 2015. I'm amazed that I attended the meeting at all, because as an architect, all we did was attend meetings. They are not my favorite things. But clarity is a favorite thing, and my self-image is also a very special thing for me. The best way to introduce my self-image is to talk a bit about my history because you have to understand where I'm coming from and why that meeting had such an impact on me.

When I was twenty-eight I had what was called at the time a "nervous breakdown." There's good news and bad news from that. The bad news is that I was a mess; the good news is that I was introduced to psychotherapy — though as one of the most reluctant patients anyone ever witnessed. I just didn't want to go through it, but for a lot of reasons I had to. And so for the next twenty years I was in intense psychotherapy — two or three sessions a week.

I had a lot of negative feelings about myself which I understand now but didn't at the time. I lost my dad when I was nine and got married when I was twenty-two. We had three children while we were still children ourselves and now we've been married sixty years. People said it wouldn't work, but it obviously has.

After a lot of inner thinking and self-understanding, I concluded that most of us want to feel good enough about ourselves so that we can better handle difficult situations. After the meeting where I heard about My Daily Rules, I took Dr. Weingarten's suggestion and I wrote down six things about myself that I really don't like. Then I practiced using the word "Stop!" The results were amazing, after only two weeks.

When I next saw Dr. Weingarten, I told him, "I don't know how to explain this, but my life has changed." He said, "What do you mean?" I said,

"Well, it's the word 'Stop!' I had never thought of using it that way." I discovered that simply "stopping" my negative behaviors was the beginning of clarity, because when you stop doing them long enough, they just go away. I was absolutely amazed at what the word "Stop!" did for me.

I'll give you an example. I went to night school for twelve years at a school of art and architecture. One of the things they do when you study architecture is to give you problems to solve and buildings to design. One of my professors looked at my work and said, "Bob, you're not an architect. You're a builder."

I was insulted. It was embarrassing. It was terrible. And I never got over that remark. But in a moment of clarity after using the word "Stop!" I realized — forty years later — that his observation was a compliment. Because architects, like all people, are not all the same. And for a builder, that was also a compliment because I do consider myself a builder. My father was a builder. He wasn't criticizing me; he was stating a fact, that I could accept myself as a builder. It's amazing how the word "Stop!" helped me to get through a perceived "insult" I'd been struggling with for decades. So I want to encourage you not to think that you've reached the end of change or the end of feeling better about yourself. It's never too late to change, to say "No" to what isn't working.

Chapter 4

Attitudes

Attitudes, which drive our thoughts and behaviors, come in two forms: Those we are consciously aware of and those we aren't. *Explicit* attitudes are ones we are consciously aware of and able to consider, for example, a belief in the value of good schooling. *Implicit* attitudes are subliminal and expressed instantaneously, leaving no time for forethought or introspection. They are triggered by internal beliefs or conditioning, that operation below our awareness, representing a kind of robot-like self that has no apparent consciousness.

An article called "The Neural Basis of Implicit Attitudes" (Stanley, Phelps, Banaji, 2008, *Association for Psychological Science*) provides experimental evidence for the duality of the two attitudes I'm discussing. It describes the amygdalae in the brain, which transmit information to the prefrontal cortex in both "instinctive time" and "conscious time." The paper also cites a number of studies, including one in which participants were flashed images of faces with different skin colors so quickly that the image was perceptible to the non-conscious mind but not the conscious mind, which takes about a half-second longer to cognify what it sees. This meant that one could react to an image without consciously knowing that the reaction was taking place. The subjects of the study were wired to an oximeter, a highly sensitive measuring device that records the amount of oxygen in the bloodstream and in body tissues, which respond virtually instantly to any changes in physical or mental activities. So as the images were rapidly flashed to the study participants, the device tracked changes in oxygen levels as the non-conscious brain reacted to them — again, without the person realizing that any such reactions were taking place.

It turned out that a high percentage of participants displayed a noticeable pattern of reaction whenever the face of a black person was flashed, which researchers attributed to some kind of conditioned prejudicial attitude. After the study, those particular subjects were asked how they felt about black people, and they denied that they had any racial prejudice. Another example of such unconscious feelings was discussed in "Hidden Motives," a 2005 episode in the PBS series titled *Scientific American Frontiers* and narrated by the actor Alan Alda. Alda interviewed experimental social psychologist Dr. Mahzarin R. Banaji about the influence of the subconscious mind on decision-making, and then participated in an exercise called the Implicit Association Test (IAT). He was shocked to discover that he had a bias toward gender roles: he associated "female" with "family" and "male" with "career." He had always thought of himself as a feminist and very sensitive to women's challenges. There is considerable evidence that unconscious patterns of emotion and belief exist in all of us — emotions and beliefs that harden into attitudes. It turns out we all are prejudiced in some way without being consciously aware of it.

These attitudes are brought about by our instinctive tendency toward fear or suspicion when faced with the unfamiliar. Our ancestors lived in tribes with people who looked very much like they did. Strangers with different skin or hair color or who spoke a different language or worshipped a different god were considered dangerous; they were unknown and therefore not to be trusted. These base instincts are no longer needed as our lives are surrounded by a rainbow spectrum of ethnicities that pose no threat to us, but the instinctive switch remains. And when those feelings and instincts are triggered, a physical reaction automatically takes place that is perceptible to the other person but not to us. It happens instantly, beneath our conscious awareness.

The strange paradox in such instant reactivity is that we are unable to perceive our own attitude. We're blind to the stance of our bodies, for instance, and the frown on our faces or the edge in our voice. But it's all too apparent to the person we're with, who becomes almost instantly aware of the attitude we're showing. One needs little more than the tiniest of clues to recognize another's attitudinal stance.

Implicit non-conscious attitudes that start as automatic expressions of anger can, for example, lead to an immediate readiness to attack the source of our anger — whether a stranger or a spouse of many years. Ancient instinctive patterns of aggression and survival are automatically aroused so that a marital spat can lead to a marital war. This extreme reactivity reflects each person's capacity for completely separate emotional responses. Instinctive reactions that happen instantaneously literally leave no time to consider other options, such as stopping oneself. Warriors have these instant instincts, which explains why, as an infantryman in the Second World War, I had no trouble attacking the enemy nor did they in attacking me. It was an automatic response. In addition, our warlike attitudes enabled us to feel good and righteous about our choices.

Two Separate Selves, Two Separate Attitudes

Why would nature have designed us to live with two sets of conflicting attitudes and behaviors — one instinctual, emotional, and spontaneous, often leading to aggressive behavior and actions, and the other more thoughtful and reasoned? Our genetic selves have been designed so that our exact physical structures, such as the complex shape, color, and function of our eyes, are present at birth without our needing to make any kind of conscious choice about them. They come into being precisely the way they are and will be for the duration of our lives.

We know from the cloning of a sheep named Dolly that her "copies" had the same physical features and the same instinctive behaviors that are unique to all sheep. Her DNA — in fact the DNA of all sheep —

makes it possible for each one to come into being as a separately predictable animal with all the natural sheep behaviors. Sheep are born with automatic counterfactual behaviors — behaviors that are fully operational even though they have never been learned. This means that sheep instinctively know exactly what to do in all stages of their lives whenever those stages occur. They don't, for example, develop sex hormones until they reach a certain age, and neither do humans.

Each phase of their life will be coordinated by their DNA so that appropriate "attitudes" leading to successful interactions with other sheep will predictably occur during the course of their lives. The sheep's primary attitude—again which is automatically expressed — has to do with herding behavior. They instinctively know, for example, that good outcomes will occur when they butt heads with other sheep at the right times. They also share a common instinct for procreation, survival, and herd protection. The story is the same no matter where in the world sheep live. Their instinctual expressions (attitudes) occur spontaneously at all stages of their development, instructed by the same DNA that is found in all living species. It's important to realize that the same instinctive/attitudinal attributes exist in both the most complex of beings as well as these simpler creatures.

The question arises as to whether human beings are, like other species, similarly programmed and largely directed by the instruction of their DNA. If so, it would mean that much of our behavior does not originate from conscious choice. When we react with behavior that is instantaneous and automatic, such as the prejudicial behaviors mentioned above, it represents a completely different mindset that exists side-by-side with our consciously caring self. *Self-awareness* is not involved. Because these behaviors are not the result of conscious choice, our DNA appears to be producing robotic responses rather than conscious choice-making. Our robotic selves and our conscious selves are clearly acting independently of each other.

I cannot overemphasize the importance of the discovery that robotic-like behavior emanates from a separate self that behaves differently, has a different function, and creates a different character that is pre-set rather than creative. We are fooled by the fact that, when looking in a mirror, we think we are seeing a single self and a single human being. Nature succeeds, however, in making our two separate selves invisible to us so we don't know they exist. When we act and behave in an unfeeling, inconsiderate, or destructive manner, it's because we become a separate, different self that's been programmed to respond as a different person with no relationship to our separate conscious self. This helps explain how people can behave with such inhumane cruelty, causing horrible damage and human pain. It's in our very nature. The powerful force of this DNA-driven self prevents most human beings from pausing long enough to connect with their conscious, compassionate, and caring selves. That's the main purpose of **My Daily Rules to Live By**: to stop damaging instinctive behaviors from being repeated. Doing so helps us to reconnect with our better self, replacing unwanted behavior with behavior that reflects a higher aspiration.

As designed by nature, we are incapable of changing these DNA-originated robotic behaviors; they are a fundamental part of us. However, they can be influenced and channeled into productive and adaptive activity. A young person with a natural talent for shooting basketballs through a hoop, for example, has a mind that somehow makes complex measurements more quickly and easily than other young people. An accomplished typist or a concert pianist has a special ability to coordinate the movements of their fingers with remarkable feeling and rapidity. This doesn't mean that such people don't work hard to be this way, only that they have an innate instinct for doing such things really well.

Ritualistic preparation is also an aspect of instinctive attitudinal expression. Football players arrive on the field in a way that bonds them together before engaging in the competition. The positive attitude of the quarterback will also influence the attitude of his team members. In the animal kingdom, a group of elephants will automatically mourn the death of a member by uttering sounds and moving their feet about in unison.

Other species shape their instinctive attitudes around their environment. For example, a dog's attitude and behavior will change when its owner walks into the kitchen and opens a bag of dog food. The dog instantly salivates, focusing entirely on satisfying its hunger; when satiated he stops. In comparison, the dog's close relative in the wild, the wolf, eats as much of its prey as it can as quickly as possible to prevent another predator from stealing it. Instinctively it also knows that finding prey is never a guarantee, so it takes full advantage whenever it has the chance. Humans have inherited some of this unconscious fear and voraciousness, eating more and faster than they generally need to in spite of the fact that no one is threatening to take their food away. As a result, obesity has become a major health issue.

The wild animal and the domesticated one behave completely differently from one another based on their experience of obtaining sustenance. Nature has recognized this and evolved completely separate responses relative to the animals' sense of survival. The dog is conscious of having had sufficient food, while the wolf can never be sure. Humans, on the other hand, may be conscious of eating "enough," but some keep eating anyway even though their survival doesn't depend on it — neither dog nor wolf. In fact, their survival can be at risk if they keep eating too much. My Daily Rules help such people become aware of their two selves: the one that knows to eat for survival and the other that doesn't know how to stop. And yet both selves are necessary.

Consider our two separate eyes, designed by our DNA to provide a stereoscopic effect that results in better vision. Working together, these two separate eyes give us a clear image of everything we are able to see, including depth perception that enables us to navigate our environment effectively. Our two eyes produce three-dimensional vision as well as a complete and single perception of the environment in which we live. The combination of two eyes producing a single, clear, in-depth perception has been provided to most species, helping them to survive in the wild while competing with other species. Until just a few thousand years ago, our ancestors were predators who needed that three-dimensional depth perception to search out prey and judge distances. In the phenomenon of evolution, each species that survives for any period of time requires the same in-depth perception of the environment from these two separate eyes. Otherwise that species would disappear. Another example: We have an ear on each side of our head to give us a 360-degree sweep of hearing that alerts us to danger that may come from any direction. Not to mention our two hands, our two feet, and so on. The phenomenon of two complementary but separate sense organs has apparently been designed by nature as a crucial feature of perception and function that has enabled individuals and species to survive.

It turns out that the same phenomenon is at work in regard to our mental attitudes and behaviors. Two separate processes of engagement — one instinctual

and the other passive but conscious — have been designed by nature to make our experience of the world
seem like a single whole while also giving us two sets
of tools for dealing with that world. Two eyes and two
ears are better than one, and so it is with our two
selves. Together they enable us to function far better
than each by itself, which is demonstrated in My Daily
Rules.

Over the past few thousand years, human beings
have become more and more consciously in charge of
the environment they live in. Human perception has
mastered three-dimensional existence, which has led to
the creation and improvement of three-dimensional
objects so that human comforts have increased dramatically. Vast improvements have also taken place in
communication and the transmission of information,
topped off by the global reach of the Internet. We've
been able to learn more and more about our world and
its inhabitants — as well as the Earth's vast energy
stores. The resources of the planet have been utilized by
humans through ingenuity and effort to create almost
anything they desired. This has meant a huge leap forward on many fronts, but at a cost: the environment is
being depleted, and much human effort has been focused on military applications and the destructive

power of large-scale weaponry. Nature has made us into separate human beings who are separate from the Earth that sustains us.

Each nucleus of the thirty-seven trillion cells that constitute our body contains twenty thousand genes and three million epigenetic switches that turn genes and groups of genes on and off. They all have separate functions, informing our cells how to develop and function. I believe that those epigenetic switches may also switch human behaviors on and off, those of both our instinctive genetic self and our conscious self, sometimes simultaneously. This may explain the transformative behavioral changes triggered by use of The Rules. The act of saying, "Stop!" may initiate an automatic switching process that is instantaneous and transformative.

When we list our damaging behaviors in Rules No. 1 and No. 2, we are listing *instinctive* behaviors, those that are produced without conscious thought. The instinctive behavior itself isn't changeable by our conscious thought, but as I've discovered with My Daily Rules, when our conscious self takes the time to consider them and the damage they've inflicted (either to ourselves or others), it creates an opportunity to stop them. Otherwise, I don't believe that human beings can control their destructive behaviors; the power of instinct is too strong. Fortunately, the power of our conscious minds is also strong. We can choose to behave differently to become a better person. Those new attitudes come naturally and unconsciously to us as we choose and act on them. The simplicity — and complexity — of this process and the role of separateness that allows such shifts to take place are reflected in how My Daily Rules work.

Time, the Amygdala, and Human Perception

The amygdalae are small, almond-shaped structures in the two temporal lobes of the brain that seem to function like their own tiny brain with a capacity to perceive and respond to stimuli in as little as one hundred milliseconds. As a separate function, they are also able to perceive a fuller picture of what is taking place by taking five hundred milliseconds. Both signals are transmitted simultaneously to the prefrontal cortex. In its fundamental role in memory creation, decision-making, and emotional reactivity, the amygdala has been found to accomplish these functions by producing separate attitudes, both implicit and explicit. In the study referred to at the beginning of this chapter, people exposed to subliminal images often had an emotional reaction to some of them even though they weren't aware of it. When asked how they felt, for example, about black people (based on data showing they reacted negatively to that image), they denied having any prejudice and were surprised to hear that they had unconsciously exhibited such an attitude.

The amygdala does its work automatically; we don't have to think consciously about what it perceives. Remarkably, neither the amygdala nor the larger brain is aware of each other. The amygdala responds to the environment in its own uniquely designed ways, each function separated by about four hundred milliseconds. This means that the amygdala reacts to stimuli before the larger brain has time to process it while also transmitting that information to the brain over those next four hundred milliseconds. We aren't consciously aware that this transmission process is taking place, however, because the time taken is nearly instantaneous. Our implicit and explicit attitudes are thus separated by nature, but we don't usually differentiate between the two. It all feels like one experience.

All living creatures have the DNA/genetic codes that enable them to respond immediately and instinctively to what is happening as it's happening in dealing with their environment. And where the stakes are high, if it's a matter of kill or be killed, this capacity is obviously a blessing. There is no need — in fact it would be counter-productive — to take any more time than a few milliseconds to react. This process of human perception has remained the same throughout the millennia. And while human beings, as co-creators of the world around them, have evolved and developed the capacity to recognize and take in far more information than any other species, their instinctive impulses don't recognize that reality has changed and so they continue to react as they always have. These impulses must somehow adapt to perceiving a world that did not exist for our primitive ancestors, who literally wouldn't recognize the world of today. There is, thus, a conflict of the senses between what our impulsive self perceives — which literally doesn't know how to appropriately interpret what's happening — and what our conscious, evolved minds see. This disconnect is at the root of the disharmony that exists in the human race. It has led us presently to two dilemmas.

The first is that we often don't know what we're doing when we do it — we are simply reacting. This benefited our ancestors, enabling them to react to potential danger instantly based only on an animal's appearance, but is not always appropriate in today's civilized world when we react to appearances without knowing what we're reacting to. The second dilemma is that the inability to accurately recognize *real* danger when encountering another person or situation can lead to bad outcomes. When we unconsciously apply the same blunt tool of recognition as our ancestors, important nuances get missed. If a person or a situation *appears* angry or threatening, we'll often react disproportionately without getting more information.

The "brain cells" of the amygdalae exist in clusters, each with thousands of connections to nerve cells and other brain cells, enabling a wide range of complex behaviors. The transmission speed of nerve impulses, however, has been measured to be as little as one hundred milliseconds, which limits the ability of the amygdala's brain cells to recognize what the amygdala's nerve receptors perceive. In other words, the amygdala reacts to its first impression of an image, which can leave out important information (e.g., the frown on your partner's face is not because they don't agree with you but because they have an upset stomach). This process is subliminal, below the threshold of human perception. It happens so rapidly that we aren't aware that it's taking place.

This phenomenon of limited, instinctual perception is common to all living creatures but in humans it has created problems. As I have discussed, we don't realize that we have two completely separate states of perception; we think that *all* of our impressions come from a single, undivided mind. These two separate states of being make us into two separate selves, and there is no way to change this process. In my work with prisoners who had committed capital crimes, I learned that murderous impulses are often driven by simplistic and immediate interpretations of an image, such as a disrespectful look on someone's face. In essence what they see is a two-dimensional image of a person (like a photo) rather than a real one. Without further information to go on — without taking the time to recognize and consider a three-dimensional person — the impulse to kill or otherwise attack or do harm comes much easier. A two-dimensional mind is unable to recognize that it's relating to a complex, three-dimensional being.

My Daily Rules to Live By

While working with large numbers of prisoners who had committed serious crimes, I found that most of them blamed the victim rather than themselves for their action. They saw the object of their rage as two-dimensional — literally like an object, or the cardboard impression of a person — instead of a real, three-dimensional individual. Such a misperception leaves one feeling no need to consciously consider a different and more sensible course of action.

We all live spontaneously and automatically, in touch with our environment as we take it in, able to absorb and respond to vast amounts of information without having to cognify it or know what we are reacting to. It's true for all species, from humans to insects (as described so well by the biologist E.O. Wilson). But this kind of perception has its limits. When we react on the basis of surface-level perceptions, we forget who we're reacting to when we react to them. When we get angry — even at those we've known and cared about in the past — those surface emotions instinctively take charge, turning the person in front of us into a two-dimensional enemy. It's no different in the tiny world of insects when they react to an intruder (although their world is essentially always two-dimensional). Fortunately, with our three-dimensional, stereoscopic vision and the capacity to consider what that ability perceives, we have access to a much wider range of consciously thought-out and rational behaviors.

And so we each have these two perceiving selves that operate within two distinctive time frames: the instinctual self that reacts in a tenth of a second and sees only a two-dimensional picture, and a more "civilized" self that sees in three dimensions but needs an extra half-second to do so. As I noted above, people aren't capable of differentiating between these two tiny time frames because they are too short to recognize as being different. And yet that very short distance in time between the instinctual self and the thoughtful self makes all the difference. My Daily Rules recognize the critical (and sometimes life-changing) need to bridge this gap by asking people to pause for a moment, list their damaging behaviors, and then commit to consciously stopping them in the future by becoming aware of them when they surface. At first this may not be easy to do.

Many people live much of their lives in a state of anger, fear, or vengeance, especially when they feel they've been wronged or disrespected in some way. This can happen between adults but often it has roots in childhood. Any discord that took place between a parent and a child, for example, expressed instinctively at that time and causing anger and hurt, usually repeats itself emotionally in adulthood with similar degrees of upset. That tension will show up again in family dynamics but can also be expressed with anyone who triggers those emotions. Thus the emphasis of *respect* in My Daily Rules, which is a reminder that everyone is essentially good and well-intentioned and therefore deserves to be respected.

In our interactions with others, we tend to see them through either a two-dimensional or three-dimensional lens — as one of two completely separate people. This helps explain why it's possible for us to hate someone we love and love someone we hate, shifting in an instant from one to the other. All of us have a potential for these automatic transformations of feeling to occur. I saw this often with couples. They would begin our sessions as enemies, instinctively reacting to the attacks they felt from each other. But as they began to practice The Rules, they would start to experience their partner as the person they first met: someone they cared about, a three-dimensional person who really did have loveable qualities. They were able to perceive each other as real people with both good and bad traits — essentially two separate selves — and realize that their relationship had fallen out of balance, with the bad overcoming the good. Successful marriages are bound to have difficulties because maintaining a healthy balance isn't always possible, but The Rules make allowances for this by stopping someone from acting on their instinctive anger or hatred. In so doing, you become a three-dimensional partner who is able to feel and express love no matter what is happening with your mate.

Whenever I asked inmates to think about why they had acted in a way that got them into prison, most pointed to problems like a bad temper or an addiction. When asked if that meant they might have two separate selves, which behaved very differently from one another, many would respond that it could be so. At this point, at least one man in each group I was seeing would blurt out, "I've been so evil!" It seemed that simply suggesting that he might be functioning as two separate selves added a new dimension to his understanding. He could now experience himself as the three-dimensional person he was *in reality*. He apparently had never realized that he was living life through a two-dimensional perspective. His behavior was evil in a particular moment of murderous intent but he had no way of seeing that he was to blame instead of the person he hurt or killed. For the first time in his life he became conscious of a larger reality, and in so doing experienced the potential for controlling his instinctive self. This is the ultimate objective of **My Daily Rules to Live By**.

After many years of facilitating this self-discovery by inmates, I found that other therapists who worked with prisoners using My Daily Rules did not have the same dramatic results. I wondered if my naturally calm and accepting temperament helped to bring this about. For several years I would keep track of many of the men I worked with who were still in prison, and they would tell me of changes taking place in their relationships with their families, such as more mutual support and understanding. Inmates and their family members were more likely to see each other as real, three-dimensional people with complex and valid emotions, rather than two-dimensional characters who owed them something. The desire for more, for retribution, puts one into a two-dimensional state and out of balance. Whenever one takes conscious time to stop the damage of the instinctive self, as happens with The Rules, reality takes charge.

In thinking about myself and my approach as a therapist, I came to understand that I always felt good whenever I was in the presence of someone I was going to help — including prisoners who had done great harm to others. I have always felt that the human race needed help and that everyone was lacking in some qualities that would enable them to have happier lives than what they were experiencing. As a child, I became very aware of the energy of violent behavior and how unnecessary those fights between my parents were, both of whom I loved. Before becoming a therapist I was fortunate to have become someone who naturally understood the importance of caring about other people. I realized that My Daily Rules are an extension of this experience; successfully applied, they can enable anyone, including therapists, to develop the temperament that I have naturally. It's not that I'm a saint, but I have found that those who really practice The Rules become better people, more generous and more caring about others, including those they don't know. This has proven to me that nearly everyone's truest desire is to be good and do good, which places them into a three-dimensional reality, making them more evolved beings, unlikely to harm or kill others except under the most threatening circumstances. This also means I have confidence in suggesting that The

Rules could help us be a race that really cares about ourselves, all other creatures, and our nurturing planet, Earth, which makes our lives possible.

Why is it that the humanity has not yet achieved this level of human potential? It's not that various approaches to controlling our minds haven't been tried. Impulse control, Cognitive Behavioral Therapy (CBT), and mindfulness training all take an important step in the right direction, but they don't include a piece that is crucial to the development of evolved, consciously-driven people: naming those behaviors that have caused damage to the self or others. My Daily Rules are unique in this respect, calling upon our three-dimensional selves to acknowledge the reality of such behaviors. Simply taking that extra half-second or more to consider the destructive actions we've taken in the past and then consciously choosing to stop them in the present-time moment of three-dimensional awareness makes the transformative difference. In this way we tap directly into our human potential to change ourselves; we become a complete person who is mindfully aware of being in reality.

In consciously stopping previous destructive behaviors, one suddenly experiences peace of mind — literally. Many of the prisoners I have worked with would happily report that, "I'm able to stop myself." Even violent criminals would tell me, "I don't feel like hurting anyone," and then add, "I am happier than I have ever been." When I asked why they didn't think of trying this before, they'd say they hadn't realized that such a simple process of stopping one's self could make them into a better person so easily.

The human race is the most evolved of all living species we know of. The twenty thousand genes of our DNA, which are 99.7 percent the same in all humans, confer the same basic expressions on all of us: anger, fear, joy, respect, jealousy, anxiety, and love. When at war with one another, humans display virtually the same viciousness as those they fight, along with a stubborn refusal to admit defeat. This is not just true on the military battlefield, but in every arena, including politics and religion. Politicians go to war in every country in the world — even democracies — in a fight to the death over policies and positions. There is no middle ground. They are right, and to disagree is to be wrong. This leaves little room for compromise or co-operation between opposing views, to the detriment of the reality of the problems their nations face. Dogma that takes the form of faith-based beliefs usually have a sameness in their advocating of humanitarian values and yet disagreements over the moral superiority of a particular faith has led to countless deaths — not just in the past, but now, whether it's acts of terrorism or the bombing of abortion clinics. I believe that My Daily Rules can help even the most extreme cases stop such behaviors if they would be willing to take the time to consider them.

Attitudes at a Higher Level

By incorporating and practicing My Daily Rules, we can move from two-dimensional, Lower-level *instinctive* perspectives into three-dimensional, Higher-level *conscious* perspectives. This evolution of perspective allows a person to live with a purpose and a caring for others, which is nature's ultimate gift. Otherwise they will simply exist in a continuously reactive state for the duration of their lives.

The natural attitude of our ancient ancestors, living in a highly predatory and competitive life-and-death world, was a readiness to kill to ensure their survival. As our genetically based species has been primarily the same for the time it has existed, that attitude hasn't changed, as our genes haven't changed. At the same time, as they evolved into tribes, those ancestors would have had to get along reasonably well with their fellow clan members to help ensure their and the group's survival. Thus, they had the same attitudes we have now, both instinctively and in their natural inclination toward decency and caring toward one another. Nature, via our amygdala, has produced these two separate attitudes by natural selection so that we are better able to survive effectively as a species. We had to be vicious in order to kill and eat and defend ourselves from enemies, but we also had to be caring and compassionate to raise our young and exist in a tribal lifestyle.

Knowing the positive attitudes we are capable of, such as those attitudes I've described thus far, reminds us of our potential for universal decency. Living longer and longer lives gives us more time to consciously choose these worthy qualities of character, making possible the attainment of our three-dimensional selves. These qualities are universal in nature. When we consider the lives of people who have gone before us, the qualities that stand out — the ones we think of as having made that person's life worthwhile — are those that enabled their true character to be expressed, the kind of qualities that are celebrated in a eulogy. These are the ones that matter.

Chapter 5

Pride

Among the seven deadly sins, which were recognized as such by Christianity two thousand years ago, pride was considered the most deadly, the one that underlies all the others. And because pride has proven to be an extremely powerful force behind humankind's instincts, it will be helpful to consider the nature of pride and its central role in a human life.

Humans are exquisitely sensitive creatures. In every interaction, whether it's with someone we know well or someone in the most minor of roles, our instinctive self is highly attuned to the prideful attitudes of anyone we encounter. If a salesperson is pleasant, for example, we are much more comfortable making our purchase. If a waitperson at a restaurant smiles and doesn't rush us, we instinctively relax and have a better time in our experience. But if they treat us with even the slightest dismissiveness, we may punish them by not leaving a tip. That same sensitivity is present when we relate to family members, especially our partners and our children. The attitude of pride is instinctive in our behaviors from birth until the end of life. It is with us for a lifetime.

When pride is felt, we experience ourselves as being in some kind of danger with whoever we're with, whatever the circumstance. Questions automatically arise: "Is the person we're with pleased with the way we are acting? Did we say the right thing? Did we dress appropriately?" We find ourselves vulnerable to perceptions of imperfection. The eighty-two-year-old man, Bob, who I quoted earlier in this book, had suffered most of his life from a feeling of having been criticized by a professor when he was twenty-two years old. He was studying architecture and the professor said, "You are not an architect, you're a builder." He didn't realize until he became aware of My Daily Rules that he could let go of his anxiety that he hadn't been doing the right thing as a student and didn't have the right skills for attending architecture school. The concern that his pride held onto for sixty years led to so much dissatisfaction that he underwent psychotherapy for many, many years to help him overcome his upset and depression. Such a simple event, leading to sixty years of deep-seated emotional trouble, shows the extraordinary power of prideful instinctive reactions.

The change that happened to Bob occurred instantly when he heard how The Rules are designed to stop damaging behaviors. He'd worked with his feelings many times in analysis but it didn't help him. In fact, the more he learned about them, the worse he felt. When he followed the directions of The Rules, however, he suddenly knew that all he had to do was "Stop!" that cycling pattern of anxiety. When he did, he automatically realized that the professor's comment was actually complimentary, not critical and demeaning. On discovering this, he experienced joy and it changed his life — the same feeling that happened with prisoners and other troubled people who worked with My Daily Rules. Stopping one's destructive behaviors in this way leads directly to a realization of three-dimensional reality.

Religious texts say that the source of pride is a feeling of superiority. It's a feeling that we are not only superior but also that we can't be wrong. It causes us to fight wars we feel we must win even when it's clear we were wrong to start them. Pride is the fearful atti- tude that robs us of so much in our lifetimes. It leads to living in a world that isn't in reality. A warrior who returns from battle brings with him an attitude of pride if he successfully killed many of the enemy. But that same pride can make him kill again, unnecessari- ly, because that conditioning is fresh; he hasn't over- come that identity as a warrior. When the warrior returns home, he has no place to put his pride, which was so powerfully present during battle. The "civilized life" doesn't feel right; life-and-death situations are no longer a daily occurrence, though he remains on alert for them.

Because feelings of danger take the form of fear, our instinctive self automatically responds protective- ly and aggressively. Pride, therefore, is able to attack instantly without any need to understand what is ac- tually going on in the person one attacks. Most killers report that their pride caused them to commit the crime, driven by the most trivial evidence of disre- spect. One prisoner I worked with walked into his cell one day, saw that his cellmate was laughing at him, and then killed him. After attending a few sessions, he came to the group one day wearing a large cross and carrying a Bible. He announced that he always wanted to be a good person; he no longer had a desire to hurt anyone. Another prisoner who killed someone who was disrespectful suggested I call The Rules "My" Daily Rules because he suddenly realized how stupid he had been to kill as a result of such a minor provocation. He attributed his stupid act as unique to himself but didn't realize that the deadly sin he had perpetrated is common to all humans in the same form of stupidity that it took in him.

Fortunately, the vast majority of us stop short of such physical violence though our minds will silently experience the rage that is generated by perceptions of disrespect and feelings of not being cared about. Such prideful reactions, when internalized in this way, are usually dismissed by the conscious mind as having never occurred. However, like other insults one has experienced but not acted upon, they join other instinctive, DNA-rooted prejudices and grievances that live on in our memory. While there they silently, almost imperceptibly, fester, wastefully generating stressful energy that has no outlet.

The strange thing about The Rules is their miraculous ability to help people shift from one self to another self; they suddenly see a reality that is not confined to one narrow focus of misunderstanding.

This is especially true for pride, which The Rules specifically list as one of humankind's most damaging behaviors and which appears to be critical in preventing personal evolution. This is a central goal of My Daily Rules: achieving an evolved state for the human race, one in which hateful, prideful, revenge-driven attitudes no longer dominate everyday human behavior, replaced instead by aware minds and a Higher-level consciousness.

In my own lifetime, I have seen my loving father sever himself completely from any contact with his brother over a disagreement he refused to explain to me. I later learned that it was a trivial matter in which the older brother held Orthodox religious Jewish beliefs whereas my father was less strict. They both were very observant of religious principles and lived good lives, but an issue that might to others seem inconsequential was enough to permanently break up their relationship. These sorts of minor differences happen frequently in virtually every family. Just recently I met a woman whose fifty-year-old daughter refuses to have anything to do with her because she feels that her mother favored her brother over her during their childhood. A lifetime of vengeful feelings prevents a daughter from having a mother and children from having a grandmother. Two brothers feel at war with one another because minor differences in religious beliefs trigger prideful instincts.

I've worked with hundreds of couples who had severe disagreements and virtually all of them were based on a prideful belief that in some way they'd been wronged by their mate. While most of these differences were trivial, the moment they came up, the attitude of each partner toward the other would change instantly. As I described earlier, I would ask such couples to first tell me what bothers them about their partner, and after both expressed their anger and frustration, I'd ask them to think about how they felt about each other when they first met. After this recollection, which of course was always positive, the tones of their voices would change and they would re-experience those original caring feelings. The pride and anger and criticism would suddenly lose energy, giving command of their relationship back to their conscious, respectful selves. Without such a shift in attitude, prideful conflicts can last for the duration of a marriage no matter how loving the relationship may have begun.

The Other Deadly Sins

Because human instincts have remained unchanged since the beginning of human existence, and because they are rooted in our DNA, pride and the other "sins" — gluttony, lust, greed, sloth, envy, and wrath — have all been present in our genetic code long before Christianity named them. Each of these instincts represents a distorted exaggeration of attitudes that in and of themselves are beneficial when experienced in moderation. Eating, for example, is necessary to survive but gluttony only emerges when we consume more food than necessary. Sexual attraction is obviously natural in human relatedness but lust throws this out of balance. A conscious pride that honors personal accomplishments is natural, but instinctive pride leads to numerous excesses and conflict and is often implicated in the expression of the other "sins." Gluttony, for example — eating more than what is healthy for us — results from a prideful instinct that we can have whatever we want when we want it, even if it makes us ill.

Lust occurs when natural physical attraction gets overcome with a selfish drive to express one's distorted desires, such as the case with pedophiles, rapists, and adulterers. Greed, the selfish desire for more, leads to cheating, robbing, and hoarding — accumulating far more than one could ever use in a lifetime while others are needy. At a societal level, this can lead to genocidal conflict, such as the excesses that triggered the French Revolution or the violent uprising of the economically less well-off Hutu in Rwanda, who vengefully attacked the more well-off Tutsis. Throughout time, greed for resources to power economies and feed a population's excesses has led bigger countries to invade smaller ones at a huge cost in lives and environmental harm.

Sloth, an instinctive expression of excessive laziness, does its greatest damage when people don't make time to help others in obvious need, including themselves. At a societal level, it means not acting to deal with such life-altering issues as climate change that could seriously affect our ability to survive in a world that keeps getting warmer.

Envy is similar to greed but is more about desiring the things that others have and can include feelings of jealousy, which can lead someone to take aggressive action against the person who has what they desire. Another instinct, which is often connected with envy, is resentment, which causes people to criticize and belittle the accomplishments and successes of others.

Wrath has also been described as anger and rage. It spontaneously brings about feelings of hatred or loathing that are experienced as uncontrollable and can lead to violent behaviors. These angry feelings can also lead to desires for revenge that can go on for centuries, carried from generation to generation, sometimes even if "vengeance" has been achieved. Wrath can also be turned against one's self in the form of addictive behaviors and suicide, though despair is the true nature of that experience.

The Destructive Power of Pride

What is the role of free will in all this? Our DNA-ruled selves do enable us to make conscious choices, even when those choices are excessive. Thus, one's free will is responsible, for example, for the alcoholic consciously choosing "one more drink" than he needs. Because he feels good as a result of having had a drink that relaxed him, he automatically has another, and then another, until he becomes unstable or drunk. Why doesn't he consciously stop himself? His pride insists that he is right in drinking too much. Getting drunk becomes instinctive, meaning the whole process takes place without one ever taking time to consider what they are doing or the long-term consequences. This is true of all addictions.

The Rules are successful because they call upon each person to use their conscious mind to acknowledge and list *all* the emotions and instinctive reactions they know have done damage to themselves and others and could do so again. The time used to think about this also enables one to distinguish between instinctive behaviors that are destructive — that may have been beneficial to our ancestors but have outlived their usefulness — and those that continue to serve us well. We still need to be alert for speeding cars when crossing a road, for example, but the threat of attack and death is very different than it was during primitive times. The world does remain a dangerous place, and our leaders are consciously aware of the threats. But war has not been the answer, however appealing it is instinctually. This is what My Daily Rules provides — insight into our motives, the damage of previous decisions, and time to consider other options. This is what we need to do for society to evolve to its higher-level potential.

Prior to Christianity, the Greeks and other cultures considered similar versions of instinctive behaviors as needing conscious control to prevent their destructive expression. In Greek mythology, for example, Odysseus excessively boasts in *The Odyssey* of having blinded Polyphemus, the man-eating Cyclops. He was punished for his pride by Polyphemus' father, Poseidon, and prevented from returning home for twenty years. A more recent example is the Treaty of Versailles at the end of World War I, which meted out excessive punishment to the Germans who lost the war. This in turn created the environment for a vengeful leader to come to power, which then led to World War II and thirty million more unnecessary deaths.

How was pride expressed in primitive tribes, which had no religious beliefs? These groups of humans joined together to compete effectively with other tribes for prey and favorable habitats. Each member of the tribe needed to work together to provide for the group and do battle as necessary with their best possible warrior effectiveness. Their collective pride instinct helped focus their strengths and energy in a superior effort to achieve necessary victories. For them, killing wasn't evil because their survival was literally at stake.

This is what I experienced when I was an infantryman in the Second World War. I saw men in my platoon give up their lives for their buddies. I had to become a warrior to support those who fought beside me. I experienced a depth of caring for those men that I still feel at the age of ninety whenever I think of my time with them. The special power of that experience is unlike anything I have ever felt — even though I hardly knew these men. This powerful pride, which enabled me to joyfully go into battle without concern for my own safety, was a transformative experience. Returning home to the more mundane challenges of day-to-day living, going from facing death every day to the routine chores of my previous life, created a profound sense of confusion in me.

For many years after I came home from the war I talked to no one about what I'd experienced. When I did think about it, I felt concern for anyone I might have killed but I didn't know how to express those feelings or whether they were normal or natural. I didn't realize at the time that this was the nature of being a warrior. By acting from a prideful instinct of great responsibility and power, soldiers risk their lives for the principles they believe in. In our case it was democracy and equality, critical motivators to understand if one is devoted to creating and living in a civilized world.

However, in my fifty-plus years of working with people (almost all of which took place after World War II), I've come to see a maladaptation in humans in which they do not perceive how they need to change if they want to live in a society where it's no longer necessary to fight for survival and procreation. When people kill out of pride alone at any sign of disrespect, it's easy to see how absurdly misplaced these motivations are. We have succeeded in creating beautiful art and constructing massive skyscrapers while also building bigger and better atomic weaponry with the power to kill millions that may be triggered by a prideful instinct. I believe that pride is the most powerful instinct because it played the biggest role in giving our ancestors the energy and strength to survive. They had to use their warrior instinct to protect themselves and hunt down prey in very harsh conditions. This warrior/survival instinct is true for all species in exactly the same form, no matter how evolved. The attitude of ants that attack another group is exactly the same as two human armies facing one another. Like tunnels built by ants, the First World War was fought in trenches built by human warriors.

I make these comparisons to show that human nature and the nature of all life forms have been necessary for evolution. In other words, human instincts have a purpose; they are not evil. However, in the absence of more thoughtful considerations, their impacts can be devastating. In seeking comfort and over-consuming, humans may have created a world that is getting too hot and depleted for their own survival. Human creativity, well-intentioned and otherwise, has led to an extraordinary level of destructiveness. Most religions have a set of principles to guide human behavior, with punishments (such as imprisonment) for those who stray, but they haven't been able to prevent the damage. We look at all the chaos taking place in today's world and feel helpless to change it into a civilized, cooperative endeavor.

Instantaneously reactive DNA behaviors are common in every area of human endeavor where competition is involved. One's ego is triggered by the pride instinct to seek ultimate rightness and domination over any competitor who must be judged as a threat and/or completely wrong. The outcome of such competitiveness usually destroys the accomplishment rather than enabling it to occur because there is little room for a co-existence of approaches and ideas. This is especially true on the political stage as even in our democracy we sink into discord instead of conscious, sensible dialogue. The United States remains locked in ideological battle across many fronts, leaving unresolved many of the great problems we see in our world today. Successful democratic governance requires a spirit of mutual self-interest and conscious rationality to energize the kinds of solutions that benefit the good of humanity regardless of nationality. Instinctual emotions, prideful resistance, and righteousness sabotage such a process, and there is no better example of the damage this causes than the terrible and unnecessary suffering of war — millions of lives lost and families destroyed over the last one hundred years alone.

President Lyndon B. Johnson, for example, was asked why he didn't stop the build-up to the Vietnam War when it was revealed that the North Vietnamese did *not* attack the United States in the Gulf of Tonkin. Johnson replied that he wouldn't let himself become the first American president to lose a war — to be "wrong." His personal pride and that of a government fearful of communist aggressions justified an escalation that took the lives of more than a million people, mostly young men but also hundreds of thousands of innocent civilians. Traumatized families were affected for generations.

Another example of prideful destruction was the Iraq War, waged by the United States because of an apparent desire to contain the aggressions of Saddam Hussein, who pridefully claimed to have weapons of mass destruction that he was willing to use, even though he did not have them. Hussein's pride opened the door to a United States response that was greatly affected by the tragedy of 9/11, a deep wound to the country's own pride. The United States wanted a reason to be aggressive, and so without fully evaluating the intelligence on those alleged atomic weapons, it instinctively invaded Iraq. And when it turned out that those weapons didn't exist, the United States didn't stop the war — ruled by pride, it simply couldn't admit to being wrong. The war dragged on for almost nine more years, with many more thousands of human casualties, American as well as Iraqi, military as well as civilian.

One of history's worst instances of human pride and needless killing occurred in World War II after Germany elected Adolf Hitler to be its leader. Even though Hitler was poorly regarded by those who knew him and poorly equipped educationally, the people elected him because he skillfully championed German pride after the loss of World War I and the humiliation of the Treaty of Versailles. He would hold huge rallies at which he would shout, "Deutschland uber alles!" meaning "Germany above all." He also preached that Germans were a super race, superior to all other humans. The German people were not only convinced by his prideful, charismatic rhetoric but supported the launch of yet another world war, one that produced more than thirty million deaths and the genocidal killing of six million Jews, who Hitler considered inferior beings. This same dismissal of essential humanity happened to Native Americans and African-Americans, who suffered greatly at the hands of ignorant, self-important white men.

Such cruelty is difficult to fathom. And yet it shows that human pride has no limits in its destructive potential. We will readily kill other humans on the primitive belief of "an eye for an eye" or as vengeful retribution or as punishment for past crimes or, most horribly, because they are different or perceived as inferior to us, making them less than human. Whenever a conflict starts between two people or two nations, human pride will keep it going because the belief of each party needs to be vindicated — at any cost. Not even death ends these cycles of conflict, focused as they are on establishing the superiority of one's position — which never resolves under such circumstances. The Israeli-Palestine conflict is a current and sorrowful example of this.

The illusion of being right also means that we must be perfect, even though our good sense tells us that in a complex world with complex encounters, this isn't possible; we can never have enough knowledge, our assumptions will always be flawed in some way. What we *can* do as human beings with our great gift of mind that nature provides is to consciously choose the wisest course of action in any situation — the one that serves the most people in the best way.

My Daily Rules are designed to make this more likely to happen. Because everyone possesses similar instincts, The Rules provide a process that anyone can use to consciously choose *humane* instinctive attitudes. When we consciously list behaviors that have done damage and need to be stopped, we find not only that the behavior stops, but that we have other, more constructive options. We discover our own good sense and creativity in choosing behaviors that make us a better person.

Nearly everyone I've encountered wants to behave in a decent manner if given the chance and the tools. But problems occur when we don't take a moment to consciously consider how to respond to a situation. In those cases, a response will be chosen for us — either humane or destructive — by our natural instinctive selves, and we won't know what role we've had in choosing that behavior when it occurs. We literally don't know what we're doing when we do it. Pride, however, will justify any behavior by making up a deceptive story in which the actor is always right.

My Daily Rules have been developed with the help of thousands of people who shared with me a desire for tools to help them stop their destructive behaviors. Our instinctive minds are similar to those of wild creatures. Our ancient ancestors lived in the same environment they did, with the same instincts and the same feelings. The only difference is that we evolved the capacity for careful conscious consideration. Other species may experience the same instincts as humans but they are completely controlled by them. Being "wild," without an evolved consciousness, they know no better.

And neither do humans when they instinctively act on their destructive impulses. They believe in that moment that it's exactly the right way — or only way — to respond to a situation. When I worked with domestic violence offenders, I discovered that the reason behind their violent physical behavior was usually a disagreement about something minor. Their pride instinct instantly launched an attack no matter the size of the perceived transgression. I was also surprised to learn that invariably they had no awareness of why their victim's behavior justified their violent response. One said he had beaten his wife because she didn't have dinner prepared when he came home from a long day at work — something she usually had ready. His instinctive rage wasn't interested in more information. Because we are conscious and able to have self-aware thoughts, we assume we should be able to resolve our disputes rationally. Our DNA-instructed selves, however, are essentially no different from other life forms. We experience similar emotions and are therefore capable of instinctively behaving wildly.

Use of My Daily Rules has demonstrated that, unlike other life forms, human beings are capable of consciously stopping the repetition of instinctively driven, damaging behaviors and spontaneously becoming the decent and humane people we desire to be. In the process of employing The Rules to guide us, we discover that they reveal to us who we are and who we have always been but didn't know was possible.

They stop our prideful behaviors and instead release newly created ones chosen by us that use pride for good, energizing us to achieve success and cooperate in ways that are constructive to human society. This demonstrates again how we operate with two separate selves. In the case of pride, our instinctive self uses it to inflict unnecessary damage; our consciously aware self must step in to stop that behavior.

Seeking Balance

Nature, through our DNA, provides us with the impulse of both wanting to be right and wanting to get things right. We are far more similar to each other than different, starting with the fact that 99.7 percent of our genes are the same in each of us. We also share the same instincts and emotions. And yet we all have prejudices, programmed over time and often against those who look or act differently from us, and those prejudices trigger our instincts. One of the functions of our amygdala is to subliminally recognize differences in skin color and other variations in appearance. This was often necessary in prehistoric times when identifying and responding to threats was a matter of life and death. Such recognition is necessarily non-conscious and happens instantly, enabling one to respond quickly to a dangerous situation with the right behavior and action — critical in a world where survival was a daily challenge.

However, in today's world, such hypersensitivity is no longer appropriate for making decisions on how to behave. We may experience prejudice because it's instinctive, but Rule No. 5 instructs us to identify and then to stop those behaviors: first when an emotional feeling such as anger is experienced, and also when it begins to lead to an aggressive action. These hypersensitive processes can cause couples to instantly and unknowingly become prejudiced against one another when the most trivial of issues arise. In Rule No. 5, The Rules ask us to never lose our respect for another person and to always assume that they are capable of goodness. This is critical if one is to be in touch with the reality of the fine and decent person they met at the beginning of their relationship. The dislikes and hatreds that trigger our instinctive and destructive behaviors often lead to divorce because we assume this "reality" can't be changed, and from a certain perspective it can't. Both partners need to stop their own damaging behavior toward the other person in order to have a decent and humane relationship together. If My Daily Rules do not result in two people getting past those destructive patterns, the problems in that partnership likely can't be remedied.

In using My Daily Rules, we open the door to our humane self, which knows how to act more consciously and compassionately and to live a better life. You see, instincts don't consider whether a situation makes sense or whether something said is honest or a lie. Whether from anger or fear, they simply react, in a flash. Instincts don't know about limits either. If someone is driven to make large amounts of money, they will do whatever it takes to accumulate it, without restriction. Basically, instincts are all about survival — whether it's the survival of a life or an idea or an objective — and all actions to achieve them feel valid and appropriate, no matter the circumstance or the damage done. This includes pride, which is akin to the survival instinct in that it triggers a protective mechanism for the ego and its beliefs. And so if we are to have successful, caring, and well-behaved lives, the pervasiveness of pride and the over-reactions of the survival instinct need to be better recognized. Each one still has a role to play, but they are not appropriate as deciding factors in our choices of how to live.

I only recall a few instances when my balanced temperament became unbalanced, and in each case I regret that I didn't have The Rules to stop myself. One of them involved revenge on a friend in college over a trivial incident that had hurt my pride. These two attitudes — revenge as a means of getting even with someone we feel has wronged us, and pride, which tells us we aren't adequate people if we don't get even for a perceived injustice — are primary in all humans and at the top of the list of destructive impulses. At the beginning of a scene in Shakespeare's *Hamlet*, the title character begins one of literature's most famous soliloquies with the question, "To be or not to be," as he muses on suicide or taking revenge for the murder of his father many years earlier. It shows that pride and revenge have no time limits when instinctively felt, enmity that can go on for many years and even generations. One of the objectives of My Daily Rules is to enable current generations to become more self-aware and discover a level of humane consciousness that will sow the seeds for future generations. Hamlet was not in touch with this consciousness, dismissing its validity as "pale," as a fog over his resolve.

At the time I took my prideful action against my friend, I did have reservations. If no one had urged or even helped me do it, I might have been able to resist — but only if I would have taken a moment to consider what I was about to do. I now know that only when I take conscious time to honestly think about my life and what is taking place do I achieve my most purposeful goals. Only when we achieve such a state of being do we truly become the better people we're capable of. Hamlet didn't reach that level of awareness, with tragic results. Yes, he had a worthy mission in taking action against his father's murderer, but relying only on his instincts of pride and righteousness hardened his revenge into the only behavior he could choose, and it resulted in his tragic death.

When we take time to consider what future reality could look and feel like, we may experience what we have forgotten: the wonder of a balanced temperament. We are able to do this because we are two separate selves, one that can remember what it saw before and another that can see something newly created. This puts us in touch with who we really are: a decent and balanced person who wants to be good and do good things in our lives.

The forgetfulness that has prevented us from experiencing life in this way occurs because we tend to focus exclusively on the immediate moment, on whatever we are paying attention to. We lose track of previous instants in time and don't consider future ones.

However, when we pause to recall the destructive behaviors of our past and the damage they have done, we create opportunities for stopping them from happening in the future. This is how one begins to achieve a balanced temperament. A different kind of consciousness is now available that can choose which behaviors to support and which to never repeat. This is the process behind Rule #3, which simply asks us to "Stop!" damaging behaviors from being repeated. When we do, our minds open to finding new behaviors that are much improved. We become a new self that is aware of its instinctive self but now consciously chooses behaviors that are kind, caring, and considerate over those in the past that were disrespectful and even cruel.

This capacity to change attitudes is available to anyone; each of us has the same ability to achieve the seemingly miraculous results I have seen in my work. The Rules could even have influenced the behaviors of our primitive ancestors who had virtually the same genetic instruction of how to behave as we do today. They did not know, as those I worked with did not know until they learned of My Daily Rules, that undesirable behaviors could be stopped so simply. Our primitive ancestors lived in circumstances where far more of their instinctive behaviors needed to be expressed for their own survival. Theoretically, some of those behaviors were needlessly destructively, and because they had virtually the same genes we have now, one could speculate that some form of the Rules could have been helpful even though our ancestors did not have the same range of options for responding to their environment as we do. It took many thousands of years for humans to evolve to the point of inventing vehicles that fly and automobiles that transport and devices that connect us with anyone on the planet and to become self-aware enough to take control of their behaviors. This is what The Rules tap into when helping people to consciously stop their destructive actions. I've shown this to be true even in prison, home to the country's most destructive people, a place with virtually no successful rehabilitative efforts or programs. Without having learned new skills or new behaviors, the majority of inmates who leave return after committing offenses similar to those that caused their initial imprisonment. But in practicing The Rules, they experience changes in their character as they get in touch with the better person that was always inside them.

As I described earlier, a good example of how this process begins is the positive changes that occur in how prisoners communicated with their families. Before The Rules, they would write letters of complaint that their families weren't giving them what they needed to live more comfortably, such as a small TV set. After The Rules and with no coaching, they realized that their families had suffered by their being in prison, that they barely had the money to survive themselves let alone enough extra to send some to prison. Their attitudes changed from blame to appreciation. I also saw this happen to inmates who no longer blamed correctional officers for their bad behavior while in prison — a change these officers noticed and claimed to have never seen in their many years of working in the system. The same transformation happened with most of the couples I worked with. Use of My Daily Rules leads people to take responsibility for their actions. This is a major step forward. Think of the positive outcomes if leaders and nations acknowledged their mistakes and resisted taking actions that harmed so many.

The Daily Rules don't impose commandments on people but provide instructions that become unique to each person's particular needs and problem behaviors.

They don't judge the instincts that have brought about those behaviors. The Rules assume that instinctive behaviors are naturally instantaneous and that people have no conscious awareness of what they are doing when they are acting on them. Instead, The Rules assume that human beings are naturally thoughtful and generous, innately wanting to be good and caring people and to do good things in their lives. Our ancestors' apparent ability to join together in tribal groups meant they had to be good to one another in order for their tribes to survive. In my own work as a psychiatrist dedicated to helping my clients improve themselves, I've been profoundly gratified to see The Rules demonstrate that virtually everyone can automatically bring about good behaviors in themselves. All they need is to consciously choose to be that better person and nature takes care of the rest, with positive changes in conscious awareness that can last a lifetime.

The Rules have demonstrated that all of us are, in reality, two separate selves, which ironically provides the insight to stop recurring patterns of destructive behaviors. We do this by stopping our damaging self, while at the same time enabling our conscious, self-willed self to take charge of who and how we are. As I've described, our instinctive self can be powerfully destructive, enabling people to be mindlessly cruel to others — even to themselves. Using The Rules puts our conscious, considerate selves in charge. The result is that we are able to become, as individuals and as a society, more joyful, accomplished, and purposefully creative in our behaviors and relations with others.

Pearls of Wisdom

Stories from Prison

Excerpted from "Nature's Best-Kept Secret,"
first published in *Noetic Now* online,
www.noetic.org

Tim, a thirty-year-old inmate who had been in prison ten years for murder and who had repeated violent incidents with other inmates and staff, began to attend one of my groups. In the third session, one of the inmates started angrily complaining about how he wanted "to get even" with an unfair staff member. Tim, who had said very little in the first two sessions, apparently had absorbed my teaching, for he turned to the angry inmate and said, "Your problem is not his unfairness. The problem is in you. It's your violent response to anyone who does anything that gets you angry. That's going to happen all your life if you don't learn to stop yourself."

Tim's discoveries had transformed his perspective. For the first time, he saw that the real source of his violence lived inside him and that it was his responsibility to control it. Knowing this, he consciously worked on taking control of his behavior and had no violent episodes during the three years I had contact with him. The last time I saw him, he told me, "I'm always able to *stop* myself. Now I'm able to help a teacher in one of the classes here in prison. I've never been happier."

In another group of violent men, a gang member named Joe, after learning about the two selves, raised a question: "How could I have believed that I was in a gang that was protecting my neighborhood from another gang, when I was actually selling them drugs and breaking their bones when they did not pay for them?" For the first time he could see that he had been motivated by a belief that all of his actions, even murder, were justified. He and other members of his gang had never known that taking time for conscious consideration of other options might have enabled them to stop destructive behaviors based on the misinformed conceptions of their instinctive Lower-level self.

Chapter 6

On Forgiveness

It is helpful to realize that many of the offenses people commonly commit are both inevitable and unintentional. Because of the pervasive nature of prideful and instinctive behaviors, emotions of all sorts — including anger and resentment — are impossible to avoid. They can quickly turn a minor misstep into a hurtful wound or any transgression into a lifelong resentment. The challenge is how to prevent such escalations from taking place. One important tool is learning how to forgive ourselves and others when a wrongdoing is committed. By failing to forgive, the painful memory of even minor events can fester in our minds for a very long time.

The power of forgiveness is that it's a voluntary act. By urging our minds and our hearts to forgive ourselves and others, we can take control of our behavior

Sol Weingarten, M.D.

and our ability to feel better. But it's not always easy. Human interaction is constant and human nature complex. We have trouble getting along because of our natural inability to control the outcomes of spontaneous interactions. It's impossible to consider, in the moment, all the ramifications of what we are saying and hearing. Differences in perspective are bound to occur and when that happens, there may be competitiveness as to who is right with little effort to learn about the other's point of view. Such conflicts are natural as no two humans are exactly the same in their thinking. In addition, nature creates unique forms of attraction and repulsion, both personality-wise and physically. Our tendency to react and speak instinctively in moments of unanticipated violation is driven by emotions that make it nearly impossible for us to anticipate the consequences of our actions.

In practicing forgiveness, then, we need to be aware of lingering emotional discomforts such as anger or shame. They alert us to the possibility that we have done something to someone or someone has done something to us that needs forgiveness. Most of these are minor events as we wonder what somebody meant, whether they were being insulting, or replay our own behaviors that were mean-spirited or might have caused a misunderstanding. Sometimes we have no way of clarifying objectively the intention of something that was said. To forgive in such a circumstance means that we give up the need to figure out what happened and simply forgive anyway. This obviously doesn't apply to *all* transgressions such as someone doing us serious physical harm or shaming us in a very public way. I'm referring to the majority of incidents, far more trivial and ultimately of little meaning, that cause us anxiety or confusion. To allow our minds to be productive in meaningful ways, it's helpful to put things in perspective, "forgive" as best as we can, and move on. Once we've done this, we can step back and consider what happened from a larger point of view. Maybe the person we thought was a friend really isn't, or perhaps it's time to consider our own hurtful behavior patterns and work on ending them.

When there's a lot at stake, the process of forgiveness is of course more challenging. Political disagreements, for example, can be especially intense with anger levels quickly rising. They have happened with me and my friends and family members and I'm sure they've happened to you. Such differences of opinion can easily polarize into one side or the other being completely right or completely wrong. In retrospect, political outcomes are never perfectly right or completely wrong. Our anxious projections of terrible outcomes are often limited by fear or inadequate knowledge, an unwillingness to consider both sides This doesn't mean we can't have strong feelings and beliefs, but if they lead to anger or hurtful behaviors, they no longer serve a useful purpose. Thus we should be more tolerant of another's position, forgiving ourselves or those with a different opinion to make room for more constructive conversations that hopefully lead to a better understanding of what is and isn't real.

In the case of war, however, the circumstances are quite different. In my experience as a soldier in World War II, killing and surviving was the primary focus of my attention. I was so intensely occupied with my role as a fighter defending the highest cause that questions of forgiveness were not appropriate. It was only after I returned home to civilized life that I was able to think back and feel the pain and regret of doing harm to others who were trying to harm me. Only then, in retrospect, was it appropriate to forgive myself and my opponent for the aggression and bitterness that is central to war. And when I finally did, I was able to heal and put an end to that unfortunate part of my life.

The Religious Emphasis on Forgiveness

Our natural instinct when someone has wronged us is to attack or punish or get even, which obviously prevents resolution from happening. These are difficult impulses to overcome, but if we don't exercise our ability to forgive ourselves and others, our minds become weighted with memories of injustice that never heal, even until our deaths. As we consider forgiveness, we should also keep in mind that the process is not always fair; we may forgive someone who has wronged us but we can't expect that they will do their part. We should not look to be treated fairly in return as a barometer of how we'll respond to someone else. We employ forgiveness to purify and liberate our own mind whether or not the offending party acknowledges what they did. We wipe clean the negative emotion. We release the burden of resentment and disagreement when we forgive.

Choosing to forgive or to ask for forgiveness is a powerful step forward in achieving peaceful relatedness that is kind and compassionate and supports a more civilized society.

To learn more about the difficulties of achieving forgiveness that is realistic and reasonable and brings out our best and the best of those with whom we are interacting, I looked to religious scriptures that seemed to affirm the wisdom we seek. In the Bible (the New International Version), for example, Jeremiah 33:8 speaks to the cleansing of wrongdoings of those who have done harm. Isaiah 1:16 mentions the process of washing and making ourselves clean as it relates to forgiveness. Colossians 3:13 suggests that we bear with one another and forgive one another. Luke 17:3-4 counsels us to forgive as many times as necessary. In the Qur'an, Surat Al-Baqara 268 speaks of the forgiving deity that pardons us and forgives us, while in Surat Ash-Shura 25 we are shown the benefits of pardoning those who do wrong.

I find that religious teachings emphasize the need to forgive because the authors knew how intense the feelings of being wronged can be and the extreme difficulty of overcoming them. When Luke suggests that acts of forgiveness may take many efforts to actually achieve — so many that it can seem unattainable — he seems to acknowledge that forgiveness can exceed the ability of our own thought processes. Emotional attachments to virtually anything, including religious beliefs, are based on personal opinions that feel 100% right. This means we find the opinions of others, similarly strongly felt, to be 100% wrong. Forgiveness is needed because the reality is usually more complex: each side is partially right and partially wrong, even when it comes to the supposed "facts" of a situation. Releasing our (or another's) need to be 100% justified in our belief is the beginning of true forgiveness.

Religious teachings also emphasize the need to forgive because other options don't work, either ethically or practically. Punishment of any kind brings about little improvement and usually begets more punishment, provoking such emotions as fear, anger, or resentment rather than thoughtful consideration of how to make peace or how to improve oneself. The idea of "an eye for an eye," for example, came from Hammurabi's Code nearly two thousand years before the Bible. It may have served the times but ultimately was felt by later religious leaders to be too harsh. It provides instant satisfaction to the person who seeks retribution but can leave a lasting wound in the other person and begin a trail of revenge. In a world that needs to be more kind, this option has the opposite effect. "Incarceration," another option that some still argue is necessary to prevent the repetition of hurtful behaviors, has not been found to be particularly effective as a deterrent or a stimulus of behavior change — certainly not as practiced in most places. If the goal is to heal or to learn from our mistakes, putting people into prisons that care little about their humanness or potential to change merely deepens the roots of negative emotions. And finally there is "forget and move on," which doesn't always work because it's never easy to let go of instances where we have been criticized or disapproved of or imagine that we were. Our minds keep hitting the replay button. A conscious choice to forgive — no matter the circumstances — is sometimes the only way to a more caring and compassionate world.

A Higher-Level Response

The Daily Rules, whose purpose is to help people create an emotionally satisfying life, emphasizes use of the word "Stop" to bring attention to whatever we perceive as a pattern of our own damaging behavior. Nature's evolutionary processes seem to welcome this telling of our mind that a change in focus will be helpful; the conscious letting go of damaging thoughts and memories helps that change to be realized. Similarly, as part of one's Daily Rules, a person could put into action the process of forgiving themselves or others for wrongs committed by simply saying "Forgive" when thinking about what happened. When our conscious mind hears

"Stop" or "Forgive," it responds to the suggestion by associating the command with defective or damaging emotions, thoughts, or behaviors, which it then takes action to correct. We have referred to this mind state as a "higher level of consciousness." We reach this higher level by removing the barriers that prevent open and direct communication with others. In the case of forgiveness, these can include anger, judgments, defensiveness, and resentments that can lose their charge when we focus our mind on "Forgive." What hopefully follows is a commitment to receive or deliver a sincere apology.

It's easy for virtually anyone to have simple misunderstandings with friends, acquaintances, and relatives in their daily interactions. This usually happens despite the fact that the purpose of these communications is usually relational or mundane as opposed to intentionally hurtful or destructive. Such difficulties can arise as soon as a difference occurs, however trivial in nature. Once negative emotions are expressed, a process is triggered that is difficult to quickly remedy or correct; we instinctively guard ourselves from slights and disapprovals. A certain amount of suspicion may be warranted given what took place, but once we add such emotions as fear and distrust, we become vulnerable to holding on to negative thinking.

When these things happen, we often judge other people's behaviors too quickly in a prejudiced manner. If we feel that someone has done us wrong, we see no need to know anything more before making a judgment. Even people on juries will display faulty prejudice in voting for punishment. The moment one has an emotional reaction, a prejudiced judgment likely is soon to follow. The rest of one's thought processes that might be open to another perspective automatically shut down. The nature of prejudice and emotional certainty is feeling 100% right in one's own mind and judging another as 100% wrong. Resolution of differing beliefs then becomes much more difficult.

When we find ourselves reaching such exaggerated and unrealistic conclusions, *The Daily Rules* suggest that we "Stop" ourselves from such negative feelings and open our minds to "Forgive" ourselves or another person. In the process of this reconsideration — especially with people we know and have history with — it's helpful to remind ourselves of the positive experiences we've had in this relationship. What have you appreciated about this other person? What have you gained or learned from knowing them? By doing this, we begin to correct our negative, exaggerated, emotionally driven appraisals and make room for true forgiveness.

It's important to remember when a wrongdoing has been committed that there are two selves inside each of us that are capable of responding: the instinctual/emotional and the conscious/thoughtful. To arrive at a truthful appraisal of what really happened, we must acknowledge and manage our instinctual self while accessing the wisdom of our conscious self. We do this by pausing, by taking time to reconsider our actions and emotions and the possibility that our assessment of a situation could be wrong. That bit of time frees our mind to function at what we call a higher level, providing a space to think more clearly and realistically about actions and consequences. When we take that time, we give ourselves more power to choose between forgiveness or mistrust, between our higher or lower levels of consciousness.

In choosing the higher level, we stop our suspicions and negative assessments which are often fed by our imaginations. Whenever we've been deceived, our survival instincts naturally kick in, protecting us by focusing first on what the other person did — on the perceived threat — rather than the bigger picture.

When our minds think clearly at a higher level of consciousness, we realize that while something harmful to us may have taken place, we can release our negative emotional attachments to the experience. This occurs because we are able to see both sides of what has occurred more objectively and from a wider perspective. By freeing ourselves of these attachments, we make space for forgiveness to resolve the negativity. When we allow ourselves to forgive or to ask for forgiveness, we release the burden of guilt, anger, regret, or shame — even if we imagine these feelings in the absence of knowing what the other person is thinking (just as they may be imaging what you might be feeling). Forgiveness allows us to move on without having to know all the answers.

Consciously Choosing Forgiveness

In considering how to improve our behaviors and become better people, the question arises as to how much free will we have. The attitudes and emotions we naturally and spontaneously express from our instinctual selves, for example, bypass free choice. They take charge of our behavior before we have a chance to consciously consider the wisdom of the expression. We do have free will and the ability to make choices, but it's only accessible through our conscious mind. The ability to forgive requires us to take the time to thoughtfully consider a given situation and the feelings we have about it, whether it's about forgiving ourselves or forgiving others, and that occurs in the conscious mind.

Forgiveness is a process that is related to behaviors that have already taken place. Nature has given us the remarkable ability to remember the details of such events, enabling us to re-evaluate and reconsider what actually happened, but this process is complex because nature has also provided a dual perspective — the instinctual and the thoughtful — which can interfere with our ability to correctly interpret those details. The result can lead to misunderstandings: We can't really know what another person was — or still is — thinking, and our own feelings are not always easy to sort out. And forgiveness is still a choice; it may not always be necessary.

We have two ways of seeing reality as well as its purposeful nature: The conditions that existed before a behavior or an action takes place, and what we might have done or should have done differently during an action and after that action is taken. This is all made possible by our conscious mind. We use our free will to assess our behaviors and judge whether forgiveness is needed. Usually it is, if for no other reason than for our own peace of mind.

Consider the case of soldiers. After returning home from life-and-death battles in foreign countries, they realize they need to adapt to a more civilized state of being. They have to play different roles. Issues of survival that were a daily struggle on the battlefield have been replaced by quite dissimilar issues. What felt like right behavior on the battlefield doesn't apply when living in a civilized environment and a shift in perspective is necessary. For many of these men and women, a process of self-forgiveness is an important part of that transition. Guilt is a common emotion for returning war veterans, and yet what they did in battle was both necessary and instinctual. The forgiving of oneself for these actions makes it easier to re-adapt to a new environment.

Choose Forgiveness

The process of choosing forgiveness brings us closer to what I call "mindful reality," a higher-level way of seeing the world that is more truthful, accurate, and open. When people experience genuine attitudes of forgiveness, of themselves or others, the weight of wrongdoings that have occurred will be lifted. This is a critical skill in a world that is full of challenging and unexpected violations, disappointments, and mistakes, a world that is getting more complex every day as knowledge expands and the human mind evolves.

I believe that our quality of life will improve if we make forgiveness a conscious and active part of the way we engage every day with the world around us. Forgiveness can be achieved by simply being clear about what we want to forgive and then instructing our minds to choose. What we found in The Daily Rules is that nature supports the usefulness of realistic tools for helping us become better people. The Rules thus suggest that we first "Stop" any pattern of emotional stress and then "Forgive" ourselves or others. As I noted earlier, there are obviously some situations where the act of forgiveness is not so straightforward, when the harmful action was especially painful. But in the natural course of everyday life, a spirit of forgiveness will, I believe, make the navigation of reality that much easier.

A counselor-friend of mine uses the acronym HEAL in his work to help his clients more easily understand and deal with difficult situations. It stands for "Hurt," "Experience," "Acceptance," and "Letting

Go." In applying HEAL to forgiveness, we start by acknowledging that all of us experience some type of pain or hurt, and that to heal from that pain, we must acknowledge the hurt, the "H," honestly. This often requires the support of another person, someone to discuss the hurt with, to ("E") experience again how it felt. This honest exploration may lead to the "A" of acceptance. Yes, this is the reality, this happened to me — or I did this to someone. But we also accept that people make mistakes, and that it doesn't stop there; it's about what we do next, how well we recover. The "L" in HEAL is the letting go. We let go of the emotions that are attached to the hurt. Whatever the negative emotion may be, we benefit from releasing ourselves from its stressful effect upon us. Only after letting go can we truly heal.

We see in all religions the great concern with the need for human forgiveness. The potential for doing wrong and being wrong appears to be virtually universal. In attempting to create a more compassionate society, what we call the "higher-level behavior" of consciously saying and choosing to "Forgive," whether it's ourselves or others, will take us that much closer to the world we want to live in.

Chapter 7

DNA in
Human Behavior

Our genes, which carry the instructions of our DNA, are responsible for every human's unique physical design. Each human fingerprint, for example, has been designed separately for each of the seven billion people on the planet. We have no role in our own physical creation. That process is controlled by the twenty thousand genes of our DNA, combinations of which show up in each of the thirty-seven trillion cells that make up our bodies. There are also four million epigenetic switches in the nucleus of each cell that turn those genes on and off (more than three thousand alone control our liver function). The actions of those switches are still being explored, including the formation of stem cells that originate the cells that make up each of our separate organs. We come into this world completely equipped with fully functional organs that operate automatically, so that if we happen to fall into a coma, the processes that keep us physically alive will continue indefinitely until the coma breaks or the body is overcome with disease or death finally takes us.

The general purpose of DNA is to design and create life forms that are able to function purposefully and automatically, enabling us, for example, to eat food, which our digestive organs break down and convert into nourishment without any need for our conscious participation in those actions. The organs of our body are programmed to perform these physiological actions accurately and continuously. Life forms that are unable to functionally adapt to Earth's conditions and competitive environment disappear along with their DNA, replaced by species with genetic improvements that give them a better chance to survive.

Our DNA also instructs the emotional awareness and expressions that we come into the world with at birth and that last throughout our lifetimes. So if our DNA supplies us with our instincts and emotions, what about free will? Our DNA also supplies us with conscious selves that I have discovered to be completely separate from our instinctive, emotionally driven selves. That conscious self is always with us, giving us the tool of recognition for how we feel and where we are in relationship to the world around us. But we don't use it unless we take the time to actually think about what we're doing. Our instinctive selves are programmed to react instantaneously so they don't need to think about their behavior in advance. This has often served us, but not when the result is unnecessary harm, which happens when they prevent us from consciously choosing more appropriate behaviors. Because the instinctive self is automatic and takes no time to consider what we are going to do, how we're going to do it, and what the consequences are going to be, we aren't consciously aware of its actions when they are happening.

This means that nature, which through DNA has been creating life on Earth for four billion years, is an evolving process that sometimes makes mistakes — and which also has the means to correct those mistakes. It would appear that evolution takes place in increments as species come and go in achieving DNA's purpose: creating functional individuals and sustainable societies of living creatures which, if one stops to think for a moment, is an incredible achievement. Still, we must realize that we are not fully evolved as a species. Nature has done what it can in giving us the tools of consciousness for living well and creating comfort and convenience — life at the top of the food chain — but human beings are still a work in progress. My Daily Rules provides a way to keep that progress going by using our free will consciousness to stop those deadly sins and other damaging behaviors from controlling our behaviors. Otherwise, the question arises as to how far the human species can continue before nature brings this "experiment" to a close.

The process of willfully deciding to change our behaviors and interrupt the instinctive response likely engages our DNA switches and other transfer agents like RNA, which means that My Daily Rules have the potential — remarkably — to improve the structure of one's genetic code. This kind of impact is the basis for the relatively new field of epigenetics and *behavioral* epigenetics, which study the impact (both short- and long-term) of environmental factors such as mental states, toxic exposure, and social status on the behavior and development of our genes and how cells express themselves. Further modifications to The Rules in years to come may thus provide even more support to the human evolutionary process. I feel that The

My Daily Rules to Live By

Rules offer the human race the opportunity to transform itself from excessive cruelty to profound kindness, which in my experience seems to be nature's purpose. That's why species historically became extinct: those that didn't work, that didn't adapt, self-destructed, making way for new and improved ones. The vast majority of species that have lived on this planet are no longer with us.

Human beings, the most evolved of all species, are uniquely qualified to escape this outcome and control their own destiny. We achieved competitive advantage over virtually all other species on the planet largely with the use of our instinctive selves, but we did not simultaneously evolve the ability to put our conscious selves in charge. The imbalance that comes from having our instinctive self in charge has led to endless unnecessary conflict — not just in wars but in many human situations — because we are behaving with the same instincts that our ancestors needed when they literally fought to survive. We now fight, for example, to get more than we need or because somebody else has more than we have, but not for survival. We are not consciously in charge when we engage in such conflicts. These irrational behaviors repeat themselves because the genes that bring them on are automatic and not based on rational thinking. What our DNA gets right is providing the kind of instincts that can create heat when it's cold, cold when it's too hot, a roof over our heads, and enough food to keep us alive, but its focus is narrow, not broad. For example, it generally doesn't consider the long-term needs of the environment for sustaining our lives and those of future generations for centuries to come. It's time to apply the same "ambition" we had to instinctively conquer other species into developing our Higher-level selves and then giving it control. If we don't, we may end up destroying our planet through weaponry or by plundering the resources that sustain us.

The Power of Reality

The vastness and diversity of our epigenetic switches and the responsiveness of our DNA are being discovered and explored at a rapid pace, revealing great potential for improving ourselves, our health, and our longevity. My Daily Rules are an important part of this process, which is the purpose of this book: to show that our conscious good selves can ultimately control the often damaging and evil behaviors of our instinctive selves. This happened in World War II with the allies' defeat of Hitler and the failure of his ambition to show that his people were a superior race — which has been realized to be a myth. Evil still exists in the world, of course, such as the horrible consequences of terrorism, but we have the tools to fight it. I believe this is so because the successful use of My Daily Rules by even very destructive people shows that a large majority of humans must be good people. When we discover the reality that there are two separate selves that make us into a single person, one that enables conscious goodness and the other that (left unchecked) is prone to evil, we realize how important it is to put our consciously good self in charge.

As I write this, I realize that humans have evolved in a highly imperfect manner. DNA doesn't easily change; it requires the extinction of most species (e.g., Neanderthals) in order to create new and better ones. Considering also what an enormous project it has been to create the universe and eventually a planet on which life could flourish and evolve, I believe that nature is purposeful, working its magic through DNA.

Evidence that nature is kind, purposeful, and intent on minimizing unnecessary harm is found, I believe, in the two separate selves it has designed in humans. During the war, one of my selves would experience intense fear as I considered the possibility of pain and death before entering battle. But once I engaged, my instinctual self kicked in, completely different from the frightened conscious self. It felt no fear; it had no concern for what might happen to my body. Even as I saw others being blown apart and feeling deeply for the loss of my friends, I had no concern for myself and even felt a surge of excitement. In speaking with my fellow soldiers after the war, some of them considered that experience of intensity to be the high point of their lives. And it's not just war that brings this out. A young man who was surfing, for example, was dragged by a shark into the ocean. Interviewed later on television, he said he felt no fear when this was happening. When he suddenly realized that his two children would be fatherless if he lost his life, he used his one free arm to keep hitting the shark's nose, causing it to release his other arm and enabling him to get back to shore. He cared about his kids but not about himself as this was happening. Whenever we face near-certain and immediate death, nature is apparently kind by making us spontaneously fearless in the process.

Nature is completely invisible to us. What we know of its actions, its creations, and how it instructs our behavior is solely through the observation of our

DNA. When we describe these actions and creations, though, we are actually describing what nature is about and the role it plays for us. In imagining what nature's "perspective" might be, then, it appears that it arises out of nothingness. Consider the relative simplicity and smallness of the original Big Bang and the impossibly huge universe it exploded into being. In pondering such a phenomenon, we become better able to imagine the miraculous reality that even though each member of the planet's population of seven billion people shares the same 99.7 percent of DNA, we are each uniquely different.

Nature's purpose may have included an "eat or be eaten" environment as part of the process of evolution that led to behaviors that became both automatic and effortless. This, I believe, would have involved the creation of DNA and a purposeful nature in our genes and cells to provide us with a body and a temperament that may reflect the character of nature itself. In looking at all I've experienced in my life, I have found that the goal seems to be that goodness and kindness are the ultimate goal and purpose of being human. In fact, I believe that whatever we face in life, nature does what it can to make it a more tolerable, caring, positive, and even exciting experience. But life is also complicated. Those who return from war, for example, and find themselves suffering from Post-Traumatic Stress Disorder (PTSD), need help in understanding that there is no longer a war to fight, that the focus has shifted to living in a civilized society. Nature did what it needed to keep soldiers alive and fighting, but then it wants them to heal and go on. They don't need to feel guilty about killing the enemy. They were simply being good soldiers, guided by instincts that are rooted in their DNA — which hasn't changed for many thousands of years. The feeling of being evil that can happen with PTSD is thus misplaced, though the difficult transition to "normal" society is very real.

Of course one doesn't need to have gone to war to experience PTSD. It happens frequently to people when they are forced to shift their perspective with no time to prepare. This happened to a client of mine mentioned earlier in the book who hadn't gotten over the accidental death of her father when she was three years old. And while she came to realize that the depression she'd been feeling for forty years wasn't realistic because her father would never come back, she acknowledged that she still dealt with it every day. I have found in my work that people react positively to discovering what is true in their life. My client listed depression in her version of My Daily Rules because it was repeatedly damaging the quality of her thinking. The trauma of a three-year-old girl losing her father was real enough, but My Daily Rules reminded her that she needed to — and could — consciously stop the feeling of depression from an event that took place forty years ago. The DNA of a three-year-old child is purposefully designed by nature to bond with its parents until it passes adolescence. When a child loses a parent, that bonding need goes unfulfilled and depression often occurs. As the child becomes an adult, it no longer needs that developmental bonding but the mind hasn't made that connection. The Rules helped my client juxtapose the separate self she was at three with her forty-three-year-old self, enabling her to see how different the two selves were. She instinctively recognized and responded to the feelings she experienced when discovering this larger reality — which is the natural response that all humans share when encountering the deeper reality of their lives. In telling me how she had been transformed by overcoming her depression, she (like many others) helped me to continue fine-tune **My Daily Rules to Live By**.

The process I'm referring to of "discovering reality" has happened throughout history. In his 1899 book *Varieties of Religious Experience*, psychologist William James presented cases from a study conducted by Stanford professor Edwin Starbuck in which people who were told they would die from their illness then had a transformative experience. Most of them had been diagnosed with cirrhosis of the liver, an incurable disease due to alcoholism. On hearing the news that there was no hope of recovery, these individuals had a religious transformative conversion, which caused them to immediately stop drinking. They spontaneously felt the need to become a better person during the time they had left to live. They became church members and followed the church's guidance, which led to an improved quality of life, far better than they would have had if they'd continued to drink.

The stopping they experienced appears to be the same kind of process that My Daily Rules evokes. Similar to those afflicted individuals a hundred years ago whose addictions led to a religious conversion, the prisoners I worked with who were addicted to drugs or alcohol found that following The Rules brought a comparable transformation to their behaviors. They lost their dependence on unhealthy substances, which made them feel good, which then brought about changes in their behavior toward others. This remarkable shift happens so naturally and spontaneously that one isn't consciously aware that such a dramatic change has taken place. The person who has been an addict and in love with whatever he's addicted to suddenly switches to another self *in that same person* who is no longer addicted. He starts caring for others and taking care of himself. He has evolved to a Higher-level self that is able to care with his mind as well as with his body. This could not have happened without the dynamic of our two separate selves.

Human beings evolve because their conscious selves, under the right circumstances, are able to recognize the actions of their instinctive selves and make different decisions. Being two selves gives us the option to literally change our minds and go from one self to the other and back again. Inmates who've had a lifetime of repeatedly being their angry self, for example, have a better self present but it's passively energized and therefore observant only and completely unengaged. The highly energized angry self is thus able to use its energy to instantly become abusive without being checked. By using The Rules, however, we can shut off the energy to this angry self. When that self is stopped, the energy becomes available to our better-behaving self. In this way we become better, complete people

Prisoners who've been murderers report that by telling themselves to "Stop!" they suddenly stop feeling like hurting anyone as they had so terribly done in the past. They still experience anger but with the least possible energy. The energy of their two selves has come into balance and they can now live with a basic calmness of attitude, taking time to consciously consider their behaviors. They are able to recognize situations that provoke anger and respond with complete respect for the other person, no matter what the situation is. The two selves are still separate but function on a completely integrated basis. This happens physiologically. When I became a "warrior self" while fighting as an infantryman, I experienced the feelings, desires, intentions, and *energy* of a warrior. My Daily Rules instruct us not to turn off the warrior self, as our survival instinct requires all the energy it needs when it needs it, but to only turn off the instinctive behaviors that damage our self or others. By discovering that we can stop the damaging behaviors of our instinctive self, we cede control to our consciously driven self and naturally become a better person.

Nature has empowered us with free will to consciously choose to be that better person I am calling our Higher-level self. In learning who and what we are *in reality*, as I've been describing in this chapter, we discover that this better person is the one we've always wanted to be. We're able to live in an extra dimension of time where we see both ourselves and others as we really are. We become genuinely caring and loving, and much less likely to choose destructive behaviors. This book provides humanity with the ability to evolve so that we no longer need to fight wars that destroy lives. We become able, as a species, to live in harmony with one another so that everyone on Earth, every nation, every religion, and every color of skin, can care about rather than destroy each other. Realizing that we have two separate selves, anyone, from children to adults, can learn how to stop their instinctive behaviors and consciously take charge of their future selves.

Chapter 8

Learning to Live in Reality

The Duality of Human Nature

During my sixty-year career as a psychiatrist, I found that nearly everyone I worked with, including patients and prisoners, observed their faulty behaviors as being "stupid." It turns out that this stupidity was actually ignorance in knowing how to act in certain situations. We act instinctively when we are emotional, such as being angry or vengeful. Our instincts rule us by making us feel that we must behave according to what they compel us to do. Those instincts come in very handy when they protect us from harm, such as jumping out of the way of an oncoming bus, but when they are in charge of our behaviors, people get hurt and we suffer the consequences.

Many inmates have been trapped by this ignorance because they didn't know a way to stop themselves before committing their crimes, blaming their victims for their behavior. Blame had the effect of absolving their actions. Never accepting blame led them to repeat their damaging behaviors, which kept sending them back to prison after they'd been released. Those who are caught in this cycle simply don't know any better. They respond to their instincts, which don't leave time for conscious thought. They didn't realize that a moment of prideful gain would result in years — and often a lifetime — in prison. The same ignorance and instincts of pride, blame, and disrespect lead to wars between nations. They cause leaders to ignore, or to not even consider, the consequences — the death and destruction that naturally follows — because they are driven by pride to believe that their side is entirely right and the other side entirely wrong. Fortunately, **My Daily Rules to Live By** enables people to behave realistically, to join their two separate selves, the reactive one and the thoughtful one, in considering how to behave and what choices make the best sense for all.

My Daily Rules to Live By

Would terrorists who wantonly kill people simply because they don't have the same religious belief be influenced by My Daily Rules to stop their murderous behaviors? I believe that at least some of them would. Because The Rules don't care about the source of or reason for damaging behaviors, they enabled many prisoners to change their behaviors for the better. In some cases these individuals left gangs even as gang leaders influenced them to cause harm to others. In Nazi Germany, Hitler's belief in Aryan superiority and the need to kill "inferior" races would have been rejected by those citizens who took the time to realize that his charismatic leadership was filled with non-sensible reasoning. Under dictatorships, people generally experience one or the other of their two separate selves: the one that accepts a leader's instructions, or the one that thoughtfully considers what's at stake and what they are actually being asked to do. Which one wins: Fear and the surrender of free will or conscious and compassionate decision-making? Those who practiced My Daily Rules would have chosen the latter, a capacity that all humans share.

I believe this is true because virtually everyone I've worked with chooses to be a good person doing good things when they follow The Rules. They discover that they have free choice and use it to stop their destructive behaviors. That decision, chosen of their own free will, proves to me that this is our natural impulse as human beings. This is what we're about. This is how our lives are purposefully to be lived. Humans were created by nature with two separate selves, one that can be good and the other that can be destructive and evil. Learning that we have these two separate selves means that nature has given us the ability to choose which one to put in charge of our lives. Those who follow My Daily Rules choose the latter. Those who don't fall under the control of both their own faulty instinctive reactions and beliefs, and those of leaders who have the ability to influence how they think.

Two Separate Selves
and Becoming a Better Person

The saying that "truth is stranger than fiction" certainly applies when we consider the nature of conscious "mind time." Simply pausing for an extra half-second provides us with enough mind time to realize that a damaging behavior we've reactively taken in the past can be stopped. It's also strange that throughout human existence no one seems to have realized that this is the ordinary way that humans behave: either instinctively, making decisions in a tenth of a second, or more thoughtfully, using an extra half-second or more to consider better alternatives. This way of behaving has remained unchanged during the entirety of our existence. Today's human cruelties have roots in the distant past when such instinctive behaviors literally could mean life or death for our ancestors.

Because this cruelty and damage have been increasingly averted during the past five thousand years as humans evolved and civilized societies took shape, we have helped ourselves in many ways. Virtually all religions have attempted to stop unnecessary human cruelty, while various psychotherapies, including psychoanalytic, family, cognitive, neo-cognitive, and neural cognitive therapies, have also been helpful. The Rules complement all of these approaches and transformational experiences. However, the world's population has increased dramatically, military technology has spread and become more sophisticated, and terrorists groups have expanded, keeping the potential for mass destruction very high. Meanwhile, individual human temperaments remain unpredictable. It is therefore imperative that humans control their destructive impulses, which is why The Rules are necessary. They not only help us to stop ourselves, but nature joins in the effort by supplying the evolutionary tools to make this possible, replacing behaviors that harm with those that are beneficial. This in turn makes us more creative and capable human beings, able to care for one another and create the kind of lives that our human nature enables us to have.

Our brain and our body are designed by our genome and its estimated twenty thousand genes. In recent years researchers have discovered that we also have an *epigenome*, made up of chemical compounds that are influenced by our habitat and lifestyle and that in turn impact the genome. Based in part on recent studies, I have theorized that the duality of the genome and the epigenome serves dual purposes that underlie the two separate selves. The genome provides us with instinctive behaviors that cannot be changed and which are 99.7 percent the same in all humans (that .03 percent difference keeps things from getting too boring!), while the epigenome provides us with variations of conscious behaviors that help us adapt to our environment and relate successfully with others.

As I discussed earlier in the book, I learned a lot about the importance of these two separate selves while working with prisoners. While teaching them to use My Daily Rules, I realized that the amygdala, which exists in both temporal lobes of the brain, transmits human thinking in two separate times: either a tenth of a second or half a second or more. Remarkably, this dual time transmission results in two separate experiences of reality: one that is virtually instantaneous and another that includes quantitative and qualitative information that provides a greater depth of understanding. This simple dichotomy leads to the existence of two sets of attitudes and behaviors. Prisoners demonstrated both of these sets, first by the action of their criminal behavior, which generally happened instantaneously and instinctively in a tenth of a second or less, and then by their response when using The Rules, which required time to think. Whenever I asked them to consider how they wanted to behave for the rest of their lives, whether or not they wanted to be good and do good, most took twenty seconds or more to thoughtfully conclude that they wanted to be better people. When I asked if the behaviors that had led to their imprisonment were those of a separate self who was being bad, most realized in simply thinking about the two questions that they really did have two separate selves. A transformative experience occurred when my two questions were juxtaposed in their minds.

Listing the emotions and behaviors that have done damage to ourselves and others in the way described by My Daily Rules, and then simply stopping them, works for everyone in the same way that it does for prisoners. This has included not only my private patients but also friends, family, and others. Virtually all of them responded with the same positive results. And there is no limit to the kinds of damaging behaviors that can be listed and, with practice, stopped, leading to a personal transformation. Because so many thousands of people have had such success, I decided to make The Rules available in this book to give everyone the same chance at changing their lives as the people who helped me develop them. The positive changes brought about by The Rules can also benefit from the support of various psychotherapies and religious counseling. Whatever route you take, the conscious understanding you'll acquire by using The Rules will accelerate your goal of becoming a better person.

Perspectives on Future Reality

In 2002 I attended a psychiatric meeting in California at which astronaut Rusty Schweickart was the keynote speaker, describing his experience of being in space.

After the meeting I asked him what feelings he remembered while in space. He described a strange experience he had when he was outside of the spaceship performing a chore. While he was finishing it and waiting until the ship was in position for him to reenter it, he found himself staring at the "tiny version" of the Earth. He said that seeing it as this small, spherical orb triggered a powerful feeling of caring for it that he had not felt before. I asked him if other astronauts had had a similar transformative experience. He thought that maybe half of them had. It seems that those who didn't were so engrossed in their work that they never stopped to experience the Earth as it existed in reality; those who did were strongly affected. The amygdala portion of the brain, which I have described earlier, takes just a tenth of a second or less to instinctively recognize and respond to its environment. For Astronaut Schweickart, the sensitivity of his amygdala allowed him to focus on his work while his other self could take the extra time to marvel at the wonder of Earth, so beautiful and tiny when seen against its vast dark background, and it changed his feelings about it.

I believe a similar effect happens to those who practice My Daily Rules, and it made me think of the experience of some of the prisoners I worked with who realized after a few moments of reflection that they really did want to be good people and do good in the world in their future lifetime. They, too, were transformed by a larger sense of reality when they took the time to observe their situation. Imagine what you would experience if seeing the Earth from space. There you were, seeing the Earth as round rather than flat and as tiny against the black immensity of space. The undeniable reality of those two perspectives could have the same transformative impact on you.

In creating our two separate selves, Nature gives us a complete experience of ordered reality. As soon as one perceives the nature of their damaging behaviors and realizes they can stop them before they occur, they experience a new reality which leads to a shift in how they see themselves and their potential. Soon they are able to stop themselves naturally and instantly. When this reality is achieved, one is no longer ruled by instinct. Instead of reacting emotionally and instinctively, our conscious self takes over the decision-making. No longer at the mercy of our instinctive selves, we will have evolved beyond where we were before using The Rules. We can change the reality in which we live by consciously deciding to stop decisions and behaviors that do damage.

Using the tools of DNA, nature has designed two separate selves so we can experience reality in both the three dimensions of space and the single dimension of time using the least possible energy. Whenever we use a large amount of energy on an instinctive action, such as becoming emotional and taking a rash action against someone, too little energy is left for our Higher-level self to interfere. We become a divided person ruled by one of our two selves instead of a whole person who enjoys a healthy balance of both. Nature has created a powerful instinctive self as a means of survival, which is why we need My Daily Rules to choose which instinctive behaviors are still necessary and useful and which are not. We will always behave instinctively and at times enjoy that ability, but when those behaviors do damage, we need to recognize and control them. We do this through the conscious self that is activated by My Daily Rules.

The opportunity I'm describing from the use of My Daily Rules calls upon us to take charge of our errant emotions so we can begin to behave in the way that nature wishes for us — as thoughtful, compassionate, loving beings. It happens when we find ourselves in the state of being a "future" separate self — the one that experiences life a half-second after our "Lower-level self" instincts have reacted. In this state we are able to call in our "Higher-level self," which is now free to respond in a more evolved way.

A 2013 study carried out by psychologists at Harvard University asked nineteen thousand people between the ages of eighteen and sixty-eight how much they saw themselves changing in the next ten years. They were asked about their habits and likes and dislikes — favorite bands and hobbies, for example. Virtually all of them stated that how they were now wouldn't change, that their preferences would stay the same. They were also asked how much they had changed over the previous ten years, and (ironically) most of them reported that a lot of change had taken place.

These findings reinforce my belief that The Rules provide a unique opportunity for people to create a different future for themselves — even those (like the prisoners) who justify their damaging behaviors and don't believe that anything can ever change. My Daily Rules do not require that people analyze their past behaviors; they only need to start new ones, using a process that gives them no time to get stuck in rationalizations.

As shown in the study, most people don't see their "future time" as changing, a reaction that is automatic. And so while The Rules focus on changing behavior in the present, they also end up changing future behavior and perceptions of reality. Humans have always had the capacity to do this, but in not having The Rules, they have not known how. There are examples of people changing a behavior (such as drinking alcohol) that they realize is hurting them, such as those shown in William James' *Varieties of Religious Experience.* They simply wake up one day and no longer feel like drinking. The people described by James also changed themselves by finding religion and becoming their Higher-level selves. As described in the study done by Edwin Starbuck at Stanford in 1899, more than 90 percent of those individuals who became devoutly religious were still that way ten years later. The same thing happened to some of the prisoners I worked with when they realized how their drug or alcohol addictions led to their crimes and subsequent imprisonment. They simply stopped themselves and were transformed in the process.

In guiding people to consciously choose different behaviors using their own willpower, My Daily Rules shows that our future self is separate from our past self. But these two selves are still a functional part of us, enabling us to recognize legitimate threats and to respond appropriately. The ability to stop ourselves from damaging behavior requires that we balance the energy of our two selves, making them equivalent. Simply saying "Stop!" reduces the energy of the behavior we are stopping and frees it up for the other self. Nature has designed us to be "good people," and the Daily Rules have been created to make that natural state possible.

We generally don't consider that each of us is composed of more than forty trillion cells that have been designed and instructed by our DNA to behave in a very specific way. They come from stem cells when we are a developing fetus in the womb and begin as virtually the same, but over time they differentiate and organize themselves to become our separate organs, which have their own cellular identity and function.

In addition, the reality of who and what we are as a human race needs to be considered against the backdrop of the fourteen billion years that the universe has been in existence. Earth was formed nearly four billion years ago and the genetic development of life began. The Earth itself is more than thirty-five million miles from its closest neighbors, Venus and Mars (depending on their orbits), which aren't hospitable to life as we know it. In our local solar system — one of countless others in a universe that extends outwards trillions of miles — only Earth has the water, elements, and temperatures needed to support a full range of life and human existence as far as we know.

Why consider these vast timeframes and enormous distances that are beyond our ability to ever travel? When we better understand the greater reality of our existence, we more easily respect our essential nature, which is part of the universe and which has been responsible for the ultimate development of life on Earth. We see this awe in the experience of astronauts who, in observing the planet from a great distance, suddenly have a deep appreciation for its unique qualities that give us life. In taking the time to perceive Earth as small and vulnerable in the vastness of space, they experienced a love for both the planet and its people. We are all a part of this reality and our lives become richer when we realize this.

I wrote this book to help people live better lives, and I plan to write another that explores the similarities between the nature of people and human consciousness and the nature of the universe. Much has been discovered and is being discovered about these mysteries of existence, which are deepening our experience of reality. In enabling us to expand our consciousness using our free will, The Rules open the door to a super-consciousness that I will describe further in the next book.

Pearls of Wisdom

From James Alexander

My name is James Alexander but my friends call me Alex. As I like to say, I am encouraged by your presence, reader. Thank you for acknowledging, by your presence, that human beings can change. Let there be no doubt. Some of us change slowly. Some of us change quickly. I had the good fortune to meet a brilliant man in the form of Dr. Weingarten who came to a very dark place, a prison, to be of help, and to share his knowledge of the human mind and human behavior with us. He believed in change and he still does.

I used to sit in my cell feeling very lonely, thinking that people had forsaken me, thinking that people had given up on me. I would feel so lonely in that little cell that I wondered, "Does anyone care about me and what's going on in my life?" Unfortunately, it's all too prevalent that people in prison are forgotten. They have so much to give and so much to share, but if it's not awakened or given an opportunity, then it probably won't happen. Let me give you a bit of my history.

At the age of seventeen I joined the U. S. Marine Corps. After spending three years there, I started hanging out with a group of Marines, one of whom turned out to be having problems with a drug dealer who came from south of the border. He asked us to help him and we decided we would. Our job was to scare the drug dealer so he'd leave our buddy alone. Unfortunately, someone handed me — the youngest, smallest guy in the room — a weapon with a hair trigger I didn't know about. When I stepped into the drug dealer's living room and saw this big guy stand up, I lifted the gun so he could see it and it went off… I'm perspiring just remembering it. And so there I was, a young man in good standing with three years of Marine Corps duty under his belt, on the guilty end of having caused a death.

A jury in San Diego listened to all the evidence and heard my commanding officers speak well about me. Three women on the jury later said they told the judge they could not find me guilty. The judge declared a mistrial and the prosecuting attorney, very upset, re-filed the charges. At the time the prosecuting attorney offered me a chance to take a plea bargain but my court-appointed defense attorney advised me not to take it. He felt that … well, I don't know what he felt. So I went to a second trial and was convicted of second-degree murder. At the time, the sentence carried fifteen years to life.

I was, by all accounts (at least according to the documents), a stellar inmate who was doing very well with no infractions, which is quite unusual. The Board of Prison Terms found me suitable for release on three different occasions, and each time the governor said no. There was no apparent reason, so I assumed it was political. It didn't help that I didn't have any money to pay costly attorneys to argue my case. The people who were in my corner didn't give up; my supporters continued to support me. However, depression set in that was so severe I started to stay in my cell.

I met Dr. Weingarten in 2008 after I had gotten my third denial from the governor. I was sitting in the front of the group and I'll never forget the moment he came in. I had the most peaceful feeling, knowing that this person was genuinely there to help. As I sat there listening to him, he said something that opened my soul and touched my heart: "Do you want to have better relationships with your family, your friends, your associates?" And I thought to myself, "Oh my god, this is what I'm looking for. This is what I want." Even if I never left prison, even if I never returned to society, I knew this is what I wanted, to have better relations." He started talking about something called "My Daily Rules to Live By." He said that we can stop our harmful impulses. And I thought about that. I thought, "Even in my depressed state I can stop that harmful impulse." I started utilizing the Rules, keeping them in mind every day. Every day.

After three sessions with Dr. Weingarten, a friend of mine connected me to a couple, Pat and her husband David. They said, "You know what? We want to help you with your education, even in prison." So they paid for me to finish my college degree. There were a lot of courses to take. In the first course I took, I got an A, and I thought to myself, "If I can get one A, I can get another A." Now, you have to remember that in state prisons, libraries are hardly on par with Harvard or Yale. But I stayed up late at night and really applied myself. I wanted to prove that their money was not spent in vain. I wanted to show everyone that, given a chance, anyone can do well.

With the help of My Daily Rules, I was able to talk with Pat and tell her very openly and honestly how much her kindness was helping me. And after I got that first A I got a second A, and then a third, and a fourth, and so on. I graduated *summa cum laude* with my bachelor's degree in psychology, all A's throughout.

After that, I said to Pat and her husband, "Pat, you and your husband benefited me so much, I want to hold on to that, I want to help others." And so I started counseling prisoners who were having problems with alcohol and drug abuse. I continued facilitating programs in the prison to help teach other inmates how to do well, to get their GED's, to do math, to learn, and to understand My Daily Rules.

My friends found another attorney who actually took my case to the state courts and then to the federal courts. Three years later, the California Court of Appeals announced that Governor Schwarzenegger had abused his discretionary powers concerning my release and after 28 years I was finally released from prison. In her conclusion about the decision, the chairperson of the Board of Prison Terms wrote that I had spent 13 years too long in prison; I was 13 years overdue for release.

And for those educational programs I developed in the prison, I was recognized in 2014 by His Holiness the Dalai Lama as an "Unsung Hero of Compassion" in an award ceremony that took place at the Ritz Carlton hotel in San Francisco. What an honor it was to walk across that stage in front of five hundred people and embrace the Dalai Lama. Wow!

After leaving prison I started working as an alcohol and drug abuse counselor in Sonoma Valley and Napa Valley in northern California. In less than two years, I was installed as the regional director of the local association of alcohol and drug abuse counselors. That was in 2014. So when I think about what is possible in a human's life, about reaching out and being of help, about the power of changing a mindset, I see Dr. Weingarten's approach as revolutionary. Given my experience with My Daily Rules and my own personal story, I believe that anyone can operate at a higher level of consciousness and it doesn't matter if you're six years old, twenty, fifty, or eighty. We don't have to settle for appreciating examples of other people doing it. Wherever you are in life, whether you're in prison or a synagogue or at work or at home, The Rules will have something for you. I can now look back on some of the difficult things that went on in my life and feel sympathy and forgiveness. No matter what I am confronted with that is difficult, I can stop myself and be positive and considerate. I can operate at a higher level.

If Dr. Weingarten's work is given widespread attention, who knows what the world will look like in another ten or twenty years, if not less? I'm so grateful to Dr. Weingarten for the transformation that took place in me. I wouldn't be here writing to you, dear reader, if I hadn't met him, and I thank you for your presence.

A Letter from Johnny

The following is a letter from a prisoner who I worked with that he sent to me on 2/26/13 when my wife died of Alzheimer's disease. He committed murder at the age of nineteen and was imprisoned in 1984 for life without parole.

Dear Dr. Weingarten,

I'd like to extend my deepest condolence for the passing of your beloved.

I too would like to welcome you back to doing your most life-changing work. Dr. Weingarten, you asked me to describe how the change occurred in me after being introduced to your concept, method, and technique of using the higher and lower level of the mind.

My light bulb moment occurred and came rather quickly when you said that one just needed to recognize and understand that there is a higher and lower mind. This *recognition* immediately led to an *understanding,* which provoked a true sense of *control,* and through control *balance* was established, laying a new foundation of mental and emotional stability.

Dr. Weingarten, my suggestion to have blank lines on **My Daily Rules to Live By** was merely just another way of allowing one to recognize (through documentation) the damaging behavior.

Dr. Weingarten, in regards to your wondering how I knew that stopping the behavior had to be done instantly and without any hesitation at all. Well, it's like dealing with chronic procrastination; one only has to start doing things the moment that you think about doing it, or when you say that you're going to do something.

Practicing **My Daily Rules to Live By** allowed me to become a practical thinker, adhering to the higher level of my mind.

My admired mentor, over the many years since you so patiently introduced me to understanding that I am my control and balance, I've incrementally taken charge of my life.

I must also convey that my creativity is now through the roof, and I now also use and view my mind as the window to the ever-expanding world of possibilities. Yes, I now live in the courage of being the person that I always wanted to be.

Thank you ever so much for all that you've done and continue to do!

May you always have the love, joy, and peace that you extend to others.

A Poem by Johnny

When we see the enemy, how often do we see ourselves?

An act of blindness that no cane or dog can assist...stumbling through a maze of fear and doubt, shouting to the heavens, what is this life all about?

And to my surprise, the heavens answered back. But it's in a whisper that only my heart can hear, and spoken in a language that only my soul can understand...

A wisdom far greater than my existence as a man; and with this timeless wisdom I disarm the enemies (fear and doubt).

And I denote the authority of responsible participation, in a new, now more overtly creative and dynamically interrelated reality that offers self-growth...

For I am the enemy no more.

References

Books

Ariely, Dan. (2008). *Predictably Irrational: The Hidden Forces that Shape Our Decisions.* New York: HarperCollins Publishers.

Banks, Syd. (1989). *In Quest of the Pearl.* Tampa: Duval-Bibb Publishing Co.

Banks, Syd. (1983). *Second Chance.* Wauwatosa, WI: Med-Psych Publications.

Barker, William P. (1966). *Everyone in the Bible.* New Jersey: Fleming H. Revell Company.

Carroll, Sean. (2010). *From Eternity to Here: The Quest for the Ultimate Theory of Time.* New York: Penguin Group Inc.

Ciba Foundation Symposium. (1993). *Experimental and Theoretical Studies of Consciousness.* New York. John Wiley & Sons Ltd.

Connick, Brian. (2001). *My 100 Days of Hell: Memories of a Prisoner of War The Story of John A. Bauer.* Waverly, IA. G&R Publishing Company.

Sol Weingarten, M.D.

Deutsch, David. (1997). *The Fabric of Reality.* New York: Penguin Books.

Farmelo, Graham. (2002). *It Must be Beautiful: Great Equations of Modern Science.* New York: Granta Books.

Feynman, Richard. (1994). *The Character of Physical Law 1994 Modern Library Edition.* New York: Random House Inc.

Fletcher, Horace. (1909). *The New Menticulture or The A-B-C of True Living.* New York. Fredrick A. Stokes Company.

Freud, Sigmund. (1899). *The Interpretation of Dreams.* New York: The MacMillan Company.

Gazzaniga, Michael S. (2011). *Who's In Charge?* New York: HarperCollins Publishers.

Gleick, James. (1992). *Genius: The Life and Science of Richard Feynman.* New York: Pantheon Books.

Goleman, Daniel. (1995). *Emotional Intelligence: Why It Can Matter More Than IQ.* New York: Bantam Books.

Gopnik, Alison. (2009). *The Philosophical Baby: What Children's Minds Tell Us About Truth, Love, and the Meaning of Life.* New York: Farrar, Straus and Giroux.

James, William. (1902). *Varieties of Religious Experience.* New York, London, Bombay, Calcutta, and Madras: Longmans, Green, And Co.

James, William. (1950). *Principles of Psychology: Volumes I and II Complete.* USA: Dover Publications Inc.

LeDoux, Joseph. (1996). *The Emotional Brain: The Mysterious Underpinnings of Emotional Life.* New York: Simon & Schuster.

LeDoux, Joseph. (2003). *Synaptic Self: How Our Brains Become Who We Are.* New York: Penguin Books.

Le Tissier, Tony. (2007). *Patton's Pawns: The 94th US Infantry Division at the Siegfried Line.* Alabama. The University of Alabama Press.

Libet, Benjamin. (2004). *Mind Time.* Cambridge, London: Harvard University Press.

Montaigne, Michel De. (1987). *The Complete Essays.* London: Penguin Books.

Penrose, Roger. (2004). *The Road to Reality: A Complete Guide to the Laws of the Universe.* New York: Alfred A. Knopf.

Penrose, Roger. (1989). *The Emperor's New Mind: Concerning Computers, Minds, and the Laws of Physics.* New York: Oxford University Press.

Pransky, George S. (1990). *Divorce Is Not the Answer.* Pennsylvania: McGraw-Hill Inc.

Ridley, Matt. (1999). *Genome: The Autobiography of a Species in 23 Chapters.* New York: Harper Collins Publishers.

Starbuck, Edwin Diller. (1901). *The Psychology of Religion.* London: Charles Scribner's Sons.

Strogatz, Steven. (2003). *Sync: The Emerging Science of Spontaneous Order.* New York: Hyperion Books.

Venter, J. Craig. (2013). *Life at the Speed of Light.* New York: Viking Penguin.

Scientific Articles

Stanley, D., Phelps, E., Banaji, M. (2008). The Neural Basis of Implicit Attitudes. *Current Directions in Psychological Science, volume 17* (issue 2). 164-170.

Quoidbach, J., Gilbert, D., Wilson, T. (2013). The End of History Illusion. *Science, volume 339.* 96-98.

Wigner, Eugene. (1960). The Unreasonable Effectiveness of Mathematics in the Natural Sciences. *Communications in Pure and Applied Mathematics, volume 13, No, I.* New York: John Wiley & Sons, Inc.

Magazine Articles

The Possibilian. (2011). The New Yorker. April 25 2011 Issue. Retrieved from thenewyorker.com/

About the Author

At the age of 18, Sol Weingarten was drafted into the Army during World War II where he fought in Germany and became a prisoner of war. During that time, he witnessed some of the most horrible behaviors humanity was capable of while gaining insights into improving human nature. That experience moved him to devote his life's work to helping people stop themselves from being cruel and destructive to one another.

He decided to become a physician and then specialized in psychiatry using both one-on-one and group therapy. For the next fifty years he worked with thousands of individuals, couples, and families in

Northern California as well as several thousand inmates in the California State prison system.

He is a long-time member of the American Medical Association and the American Psychiatric Association. In 2011 he published an article entitled "Nature's Best-Kept Secret" that first described the technique he presents more fully in this book. More information can be found on his website, www.solweingarten.com, and there are plans for a second book that will offer more help and understanding about the conscious aspects of human behavior. Dr. Weingarten is retired from practice and lives in the San Francisco Bay Area.

Made in the USA
San Bernardino, CA
23 March 2019